the AMAZING TREAT DIET FOR DOGS

How I Saved My Dog From Obesity

the AMAZING TREAT DIET FOR DOGS

How I Saved My Dog From Obesity

by **KATIE NEWMAN**

The ideas, methods and suggestions contained in this book are not intended as a substitute for consulting with your veterinarian. The advice and strategies contained herein may not be suitable for every situation. Neither the author nor the publisher shall be liable or responsible for any loss or damage allegedly arising from any information or recommendations in this book.

Published by Pomp Productions, LLC
4570 Van Nuys Blvd PMB #183
Sherman Oaks, California 91403-2913

www.AmazingTreatDiet.com

First printing, July 2011

Book design by Andras Kanegson
Cover design by Michael Newman
Photography by Katie and Michael Newman

TO MY TWO BEST FRIENDS
my husband, Michael, and our dog, Hustler.

AND TO ALL DOGS
may you live long, happy and healthy lives!

Table of Contents

Starting Your Dog on The Amazing Treat Diet

Appendix

Introduction

When I first developed this diet, the thought of writing a doggy diet book never crossed my mind. I had one goal: to help my pup lose weight.

Sounds easy, right? It wasn't. My dog Hustler suffered from numerous ailments, which made normal canine activity impossible. Months of a sedentary lifestyle led to a lot of extra pounds. I didn't realize how big he had become until a fateful vet visit.

I wracked my brain for a solution to Hustler's problem. After countless hours of research and planning, I formulated *The Amazing Treat Diet for Dogs.* Within four months Hustler was at his ideal weight, which he has maintained for over a year.

According to The Association for Pet Obesity Prevention, over 50% of dogs in the U.S. are overweight or obese. Many of these portly pooches have other medical difficulties which restrict exercise, making weight loss a huge challenge.

I wrote this book to share what we went through and to help other people and their dogs who experience similar obstacles to good health.

How To Use This Book

This book will save your dog.

Our Story is the story of how the diet began, from the first to the last weigh-in. As you read our amusing and heartening tale, you will learn key diet principles and how weight truly affects dogs.

Starting Your Dog on The Amazing Treat Diet contains the diet guidelines you need to know – Everything from what to and what not to feed, along with important dog health information.

The *Appendix* contains supplemental reference data and helpful charts to reference throughout your dog's journey to better health.

The Amazing Treat Diet for Dogs is intended for healthy dogs with normal digestive tracts. Consult your veterinarian before making any changes to your dog's diet.

Our Story

I Fat and...Happy?

1   Meet Hustler

In March 2004, a local Florida newspaper ran a classified ad entitled *Fat and Happy Labrador Retriever Pups.* My husband Michael responded to the ad and we took a long drive out to the country home. We greeted an older gentleman in a flannel shirt, who ushered us to the litter of sleeping, four-week-old yellow and chocolate Labs. One puppy stirred at the sound of my voice. I picked him up and gingerly held him in my arms. He winced at the bright sun, but licked my nose and nestled his head against my cheek. That was the moment I knew the fat pup would join our family. The only thing he needed was a name. Since my husband and I are billiard enthusiasts with the last name *Newman*, we knew… we named him Hustler.

Since Hustler was too young to be separated from his mother, we scheduled visits over the next four weeks. It was great to see him. But it was tough when it came time to leave without him. Between visits, I read puppy training books and filled the house with stuffed toys, balls and dog pillows. On our last visit, Hustler ran toward me and jumped in my arms, as if he knew he could finally come home. Instantly, my life changed. I became a mother, and Hustler was my not-so-little bundle.

Hustler shed his puppy flab and grew into a healthy, athletic dog. At 12 weeks, he had his first ocean swim and, at 22 weeks, he jumped his first hurdle in a backyard agility course my husband had built. Whether we were discovering trails, climbing hills or traveling across the country, every day was an adventure. The word *fat* was no longer an appropriate description for Hustler, but was used jokingly in our *how we met* story.

A year later, we left sunny Florida and moved to even sunnier Los Angeles, where Hustler enjoyed many long afternoon walks and the occasional swim in the Pacific. He quickly became popular in our neighborhood, somewhat of a *top dog.* Cars honked as they passed, no doubt from drivers charmed by Hustler's charismatic smile. He swaggered as if the sidewalk was a doggy runway, his tail jutting side-to-side like a model's fierce strut. We'd meet up with other dogs on walks and everyone loved him, canine and human alike. Our life with Hustler was fantastically free of troubles, until February 2008, when a clumsy step off a curb resulted in what we assumed would be a routine vet visit.

Since Hustler appeared to be in good overall health, the vet concluded that the limp was no more than a strained muscle that would be fine after several restful days. After two weeks, his limp was gone and he was back to his old, playfully goofy self. However, during the months that followed, the limp resurfaced after every ocean swim, so we stopped going to the beach. One afternoon, after only a few blocks, he began walking very slowly. When I looked down, I noticed his front left leg was stilted to support his right elbow, which was swollen. By the time we came home, his entire right side was lame and he couldn't walk up the stairs. As I struggled to carry him, he whimpered for the first time. It broke my heart to hear him in pain. A week later, our vet served up a new diagnosis: bilateral elbow and hip dysplasia, with a side order of degenerative arthritis.

Over the next year, Hustler's condition worsened. Park walks, which had brought him so much joy in the past, became painful reminders he could no longer play with his friends. He would sit quietly and watch as other dogs chased each other and caught tennis balls, with a *why can't that be me, mommy?* expression. Even if we were just walking down the street, it seemed there was always a dog running beside a skateboard or bicycle, and Hustler would be once again reminded of his former life.

Since he could still swim in gentle water, we moved into a house with a backyard pool. Within a week, we learned that swimming longer than 20 minutes caused a painful limp, requiring an anti-inflammatory shot. As Hustler's physical activity waned, his boredom grew. At first, he tried to get our attention, dropping a ball at our feet, hoping to engage in the same games he used to play. Eventually, he became listless, spending hours staring at the movements of the world outside the window. To solve this problem, my husband invented a low-impact fetch game that could be used indoors. Although beach and travel gear were stored away, Hustler, equipped with The Amazing Treat Machine *(see below)*, was entertained.

THE AMAZING TREAT MACHINE *by Michael Newman*

Hustler had, as the doctor put it, three and a half bad legs, and was no longer allowed to play his favorite game, fetch. I wondered if there was a way for him to get enjoyment out of his beloved tennis balls, other than chewing them or retrieving them during the occasional swim.

Supplied with a tennis ball and a pocketful of dog food, I stalked the aisles of our local hardware store. I rolled the ball through pipes and shook dog food out of mesh screens. After an hour of impromptu experimentation (and a lot of odd looks), I left with three bags of stuff.

We spent the better part of four days assembling various Rube Goldberg-style contraptions. I built, Hustler tested, until we found the perfect combination of a bucket, PVC pipes, a big cardboard box and lots of tape to hold everything together. He dropped the ball in. The ball and treats came out. Hustler was overjoyed, and I was exhausted but happy to see my pup engaged and amused.

While Hustler adjusted to his new lifestyle, I researched joint and limb surgical treatments. I was very excited to discuss our options at our annual vet exam. We entered the office in the hope of repairing nature's cruel flaws. Then, Hustler stepped on the scale.

96 lbs.

Our vet, who could stand to lose a few pounds herself, chuckled while giving him a new nickname. *Sausage.* I was mortified. At five years old, Hustler had become a statistic. He was fat. I could no longer say *he's just big boned.*

I swallowed my pride and asked how to *fix* Hustler's problem, as if a fairy could just sprinkle glittery weight-loss dust on him. In retrospect, my vet probably thought I was completely oblivious, but to soften my embarrassment, she assured me it was a common question.

While she pinched Hustler's fat cheeks and uttered a steady stream of annoying baby talk, she cautioned me about life threatening health conditions caused by obesity. As if having four bad legs wasn't enough, he was now at very serious risk for incurable diseases, such as cancer. She rubbed his fat belly and said to him: *You need to eat less. You need to exercise more... oh, not in your case. And, of course, you can't have anymore treats.*

No treats? I gasped. I repeated the words as I shook my head. It was an obvious and practical recommendation, but dogs understand behavior, not logic. *Would he think he was being punished?* I concluded Hustler would not be very accepting of a meals only diet. Food isn't love, of course, but we used treats as rewards to reinforce good behavior.

As we left the vet, I tried to reconcile her advice and what I thought was best for Hustler. But as I watched him waddle to the car, I knew that she was right about one thing. *Fat* was once again an appropriate description, and one that he desperately needed to shed.

2 Sausage 101

It's been over a year since that fateful visit to the vet. I still ask myself how I didn't realize Hustler had grown so fat that his body resembled a tube of processed meat. Why didn't I recognize his extreme weight problem when the media bombards us with articles about pet obesity? Probably because it didn't happen overnight. He also wasn't rolly-polly fat. His extra weight took on a solid mass that circled his torso and looked, dare I say, *naturally* stout.

Friends, family members and even fellow dog parents had dropped numerous subtle and not-so-subtle hints. My favorites include:
... *What a BIG boy he is now!*
... *He certainly must get a lot of couch time!*
... *Someone is well fed...*
... *Is he STILL growing?*
... *He really likes his treats, huh?*
... *Is there any Saint Bernard in him?* This is only comical when your dog's breed in no way resembles a Saint Bernard.

How did I overlook that his torso grew to resemble Sasquatch? Perhaps because I was focusing on what was happening *below* his belly. I would look past the rest of him and see only his damaged legs, turning a blind eye to the fact that he was growing daily. Slip and falls had become so common, Hustler was almost exclusively confined to his pillow, which hid much of the fat. Sometimes I wonder if I unconsciously chose to ignore his weight and still see him the way he was.

My reasons for allowing Hustler's weight gain are not justifications or a misguided attempt to atone for his condition. People instinctively deconstruct problems to discover solutions, but, trust me, attempting to understand *how* your dog became overweight is irrelevant and exhausting. Instead, you absolutely need to determine just how fat you let your dog become, which can be emotionally difficult. *Obese* is such a heinous word, especially when used to describe your best friend.

Hustler was once muscular, so his body size didn't drastically change. There was just more wiggle. Some dogs' builds make it difficult to tell the difference between being overweight and obese. Reports indicate many owners don't know their dogs' weights have reached unhealthy levels. Even we humans have a tough time making the distinction with our own bodies. However, there is a clinical difference, as applicable for dogs as it is for us non-canines. Many accredited organizations list healthy weight ranges for all breeds, however the ranges are often broad and independent of other factors, such as height and muscle tone. The best way to know if your dog is overweight or obese is by examining his or her body, specifically the waistline.

Overweight: weight over and above what is required or allowed. 5-10% over ideal weight.
Body Conditioning Score: Level 4 *(see following chart)*

Obese: having excessive body fat.
11% or higher over ideal weight. (Hustler was 26% over ideal weight)
Body Conditioning Score: Level 5 *(see following chart)*

BODY CONDITIONING SCORING (BCS) CHART

(Descriptions published by The Association For Pet Obesity Prevention)

1 Emaciated, bony and starved in appearance.
Ribs, spine and bony protrusions are easily seen at a distance. These dogs have lost muscle mass and there is no observable body fat.

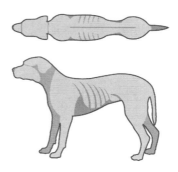

2 Thin, lean or skinny in appearance.
Ribs, spine and other bones are easily felt. These dogs have an obvious waist when viewed from above and an abdominal tuck.

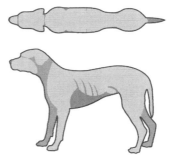

3 Normal, ideal and often muscular in appearance.
Ribs and spine are easily felt but not necessarily seen. There is a waist when viewed from above and the abdomen is raised and not sagging when viewed from the side.

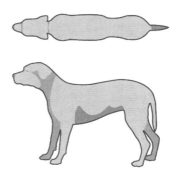

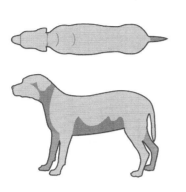

4 Overweight, heavy, husky or stout.

Ribs and spine are hard to feel or count underneath fat deposits. Waist is distended or often pear-shaped when viewed from above. The abdomen sags when seen from the side. There are typically fat deposits on the hips, base of tail and chest.

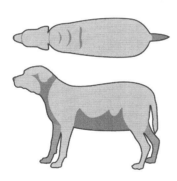

5 Obese *(or Sausage).*

Large fat deposits over the chest, back, tail base and hindquarters. The abdomen sags prominently and there is no waist when viewed from above. The chest and abdomen often appear distended or swollen.

Until I looked down and saw that Hustler's tucked out waist was wider than his head, I really didn't think he was, well, *that* fat. From a side view, he had certainly gained some weight, but I thought it was just a few extra pounds. As I grabbed handfuls of excess fat around his ribs, it was immediately undeniable. He had a waist like the Hindenburg, and according to the body conditioning scoring chart, had become a certified, Level 5 Sausage.

3   Painful Pounds

Obesity put Hustler at major risk for many ailments, including diabetes, kidney disease, and heart and respiratory diseases, not to mention decreased life expectancy. Although these are very serious health conditions, my concern was not with down-the-road scenarios. I needed to focus on what was in front of me. One afternoon, while drying Hustler off after a swim, I could feel his hip bones grind against each other as he moved. There was no longer cartilage left to cushion his joint, new misshapen bone had formed, and his hips were progressively deteriorating.

I sincerely hope your dog's name is never spoken in the same sentence as *dysplasia*, *arthritis*, or *coronoid fragmentation*. If it is, although weight does not cause these serious health conditions, it is important to know that it greatly affects them. Each pound adds pain and severely restricts movement. For dogs suffering from these often hereditary conditions, there are no cures, only surgical and non-surgical treatments, and pain management. The best non-surgical treatment you can provide your dog is a healthy weight.

Have you ever baked a cake? Imagine strapping five 5 lbs bags of flour to a dog whose legs are connected to misaligned hips. Or imagine your dog carrying a two year old on his or her back with front elbows encased by floating bone fragments.

Part of the problem with determining a dog's ideal weight lies in our understanding of what a pound *means*. An extra pound of weight on a human could equate to two, four, or even more for your dog, depending on his or her breed. To illustrate this point, let's take Hustler as an example. If, for instance, Hustler's ideal weight is 69 lbs, let's think of a person whose ideal weight is twice that (138 lbs). Hustler weighed 96 lbs at his heaviest, 27 lbs over ideal. That would be equivalent to that 138 lbs person tipping the scales at 192 lbs!

I would like to stress that Hustler's incurable osteopathic conditions were not caused by obesity. Following his diagnoses, I attempted to reduce Hustler's exercise. I shortened ball throwing distances so he could still play fetch, until one morning when he cried chasing after a grounded ball. Whether or not the excess weight led to more rapid bone degeneration, I will never know. But after witnessing his mobility dramatically decline, I believe his limbs would be stronger today if he never carried that extra weight.

Every dog needs exercise. Although this diet does not *require* exercise, if your dog is able to walk, then get out there. Your dog deserves to have the quality of life you always wanted for him or her. In an ideal world, every dog's limbs would be strong enough for intense cardio workouts and playtimes. Hustler is no longer able to run or go on extended walks, but we will often spend an hour sitting curbside. It's not a dog's paradise, but it beats staying inside.

4　What's In The Bowl?

Your dog's diet is decided by you. Unlike people struggling with diets, your dog isn't sneaking into the fridge for ice cream. Understand *you* are the reason your dog is fat. I caused Hustler's obesity and was determined to correct my mistakes. Hustler needed hip surgery and obesity made him an undesirable candidate. It was a war against weight, a battle to wipe out Hustler's pain, and our enemies were kibble and biscuits.

Before I was going to alter any part of Hustler's diet, I needed to identify how these culprits, *ahem,* weighed-in. With trusty pen and paper in hand, I recorded everything he ate for the next 48 hours, including the itty-bitty scraps.

Forty-eight hours later, my list was complete. Hustler received:

- kibble servings as recommended by manufacturer labels
- low-fat treats
- a few bites of boiled chicken to reinforce leash-training exercises

What's your dog eating?

✎ To better understand your pooch's present diet, write down what he or she eats during the next 48 hours.

I read it, analyzed it, but didn't see anything *wrong* with it. Food quantities did not appear excessive, yet white, fluffy rolls of fat spilled over his hips. It was time to look at the *quality* of what he was eating, which can be very difficult depending on who you ask.

I know from experience there are countless brands of commercial dog food, homemade diets, special supplements, et cetera. Investigating all the canine feeding options is a daunting proposition. I had always fed Hustler dry kibble because it is what his vets recommend, however I have many friends that feed their dogs canned, pouched and raw food. I have never pursued a raw food diet or strictly homemade diet mainly because of the time and resources it requires.

When choosing between the types of food available, I strongly recommend you decide with your vet what is best for you and your dog. Your dog may have special dietary needs, allergies or certain health issues that require very specific food. Whether you chose wet or dry food is your decision, but you should chose a brand that you believe offers quality ingredients.

If you are unsure what's actually in your dog's food, I suggest a quick Internet search among kibble companies to compare ingredients. Many companies have checklists, charts or abbreviated ingredients lists. If you're thinking about changing your dog's commercial food, give your vet a call and discuss it, as there are some popular manufacturers that have a long history of product recalls. For a comprehensive list of current recalls, search the U.S. Food and Drug Administration website.

Once, I gave in to a clever advertising campaign and fed Hustler the premium, colorful kibble depicted in the ad, only to learn it caused crystals in his urine. Luckily, we discovered the crystals before bladder stones developed, switched kibble and he was fine. I quickly discovered that major brands don't always offer the best food, even if the commercial is well produced.

Growing up, we always had a dog in the house, along with rabbits, hamsters, rodents and fish. My mother didn't earn a lot of money. Our dogs were fed economical food that required a can opener. I've fed dogs manufactured foods ranging from bargain generic canned to prescription dry and wet. My childhood beagle-mix, Missy, ate bottom shelf canned food and lived 17 years!

Many health books have been published to offer dog parents helpful advice and facts. After looking into several popular publications, I chose one readily available. *The Dog Bible*, by Tracie Hotchner, is a great resource to grab for non-emergency advice. Hotchner compiles a comprehensive list of what to avoid in dog foods:

By-Products (Meat or Poultry) indicate a lower-quality dry dog food. They have nutritional value but less than meat or meat meal, which are more expensive and handled more carefully.

Fats or proteins from unknown sources. "Animal fat" is a catch phrase that can include low-quality, inexpensive fats from source, even including old restaurant grease.

"Dedicated fiber sources" are less desirable because they are by-products of other food manufacturing processes.

Crude protein is not an ingredient that a dog's body can utilize. It is not what most people would even think of as protein, since it refers to beaks, hairs, hooves, feathers and tendons.

"Powdered cellulose" is the fiber source with the lowest value of all. It is defined by the AAFCO (Association of American Feed Control Officials) as "purified, mechanically disintegrated cellulose prepared by processing alpha cellulose obtained as pulp from fibrous plant materials." A less fancy description is "sawdust."

Artificial colors or flavors are unhealthy chemicals, which can have long-term health consequences and should not be necessary to entice a dog when the food has good quality ingredients. Colors are meaningless to a dog but are used to attract the human buyer.

Sugar or other sweeteners. Cheap dog foods use sweeteners (corn syrup, sucrose and ammoniated glycyrrhizin) because dogs have a sweet tooth. Sugar in the diet can aggravate health problems like diabetes in dogs.

Food fragments are lower-cost by-products that come from processing another food, for example wheat bran, which is what's left after the nutritious wheat kernel is removed. Many products have some food fragments, but look out for multiple fragments from one food – which is a way to hide a large amount of a low-value ingredient. For example, a food that lists corn in various forms has a lot more corn than it does meat protein, which may therefore deceptively appear first on the ingredient list.

Flavor and texture enhancers. If food is made of good ingredients, it shouldn't be necessary to boost it with any additives.

Hustler's food was dry premium kibble that scored well on Hotchner's list. He received the correct amounts according to labels. The biscuits were low-fat, and he sometimes received boiled chicken and cooked liver. It wasn't a diet filled with table scraps and pizza, or any processed human food, but the scale demanded change. *Something* was being overlooked and I was determined to know what.

5 Count Your Kibble

Days passed as we sat, huddled in front of a computer screen. Everything I read about dog weight loss said to feed less and exercise more. But I knew figuring out a way for Hustler to still enjoy treats had to be possible. I kept reminding myself there is always a solution, it just required ingenuity and inspiration, which lay asleep at my feet.

In reading about obesity, I learned more than I wanted to know about his joint conditions and how even a few extra pounds cause agonizing pain. Each day that I placed bowls of kibble on the floor and rang Hustler's dinner bell, I felt horrible, knowing I was adding more weight, which meant more pain. It was time to confront the enemy in our pantry.

That afternoon, I read the feeding instructions for Hustler's dry kibble. Three and a half to four 8 ounce cups per day. Easy, right? I *thought* so. But then I realized my first mistake. At the time, I was feeding him the amount listed for dogs *over* 80 lbs because he weighed 96 lbs. He should have been fed the amount for his ideal weight, which is well under 80 lbs. It was a *what was I thinking* moment, humbling but necessary. This simple recognition helped transform Hustler's unhealthy diet into a healthy one.

It's important to note information gathered online requires a shovel, sometimes a jumpsuit, to sift through the heap. If you are doing an Internet search on your dog's healthy weight range, be very careful. Your dog's weight is also determined by height. You should speak to your vet before deciding what is ideal for your dog. I learned that a male Labrador Retriever's weight can healthily range between 60-80 lbs, a range as large and robust as Hustler's pre-diet buttocks!

What's your pup's ideal weight range?
✎ Your vet can help you identify your dog's ideal weight range. If you have a purebred the American Kennel Club website lists breed information along with average size and weight ranges

In feeding him the recommended amount for 80+ lbs dogs, he was already receiving an excessive ½ cup (4 ounces) of kibble. That's over 200 calories per day!

If you think I just started feeding Hustler the correct amount of kibble according to his proper weight range and 27 lbs came off in less than five months, then you are incorrect. It would have been a good start, but in no way would it have resulted in dramatic weight loss. Weight is an intimidating opponent and your dog's health demands you duel, so engage with courage, determination and, in this case, a calculator.

According to the commercial food label, one serving of 3-3½ cups would be the proper daily feeding portion for Hustler's ideal weight range (60-80 lbs), yet the calories seemed high. The Association for Pet Obesity Prevention lists the daily caloric guidelines for average, lightly active adult spayed/neutered dogs (one to seven years old), receiving less than 30 minutes of aerobic activity per day, as:

10 lbs dogs – 200 to 275 calories
20 lbs dogs – 325 to 400 calories
50 lbs dogs – 700 to 900 calories

What's your pup's ideal daily caloric intake?

✐ Since caloric needs of a particular canine may differ depending on such factors as lifestyle, genetics, activity level and medical conditions, it is important to identify your dog's daily needs with your veterinarian.

Even if Hustler was at an ideal weight, I knew he should receive more than 900 calories per day. For dogs between 20-50 lbs, the calories increased by 100 per 10 lbs. So, I concluded 1100 calories per day would be a good starting point.

> 900 calories (50 lbs)
> + 100 calories (10 lbs)
> + 100 calories (10 lbs)
> _____
> 1100 calories for a 70 lbs weight goal!

At the time, I never imagined Hustler would actually weigh in at 70 lbs. But I knew if I started feeding him like a 70 lbs dog should be fed, then he would get closer to that goal. Based on an 1100 calorie diet, I returned to further inspect the dry food bag label.

For his ideal weight the kibble company recommends:
🦴 3-3½ cups daily
🦴 1 cup (8 oz) contains 463 calories

Even if I stuck to the lower amount and only fed Hustler 3 cups per day, he would still receive 1,389 calories daily, leaving absolutely no room for treats! If I combined kibble reduction and also reduced his biscuit intake by half, then Hustler would still consume 1,789 calories daily (1,389 from kibble, 400 from biscuits).

No wonder he plumped up into a little piggy! After these calculations, I needed more than articles and advice suggesting cutting back on kibble and treats. To put myself in Hustler's paws, I measured 3 cups of food and wondered whether the amount would satisfy me for a 24-hour period. Hearing me scoop kibble, Hustler came wagging in.

I asked him how he felt about the measurement. He quietly retreated to his pillow with his proverbial tail between his legs.

After skimming recipes and rigid diets, some of which require extensive preparation and expensive ingredients, I knew I needed another answer. Sure, there are thousands of special food and doggy diet books on the shelves. I spent days searching online, reading articles and watching infomercials promoting canine meal programs. I even looked into a few, but ingredients such as olive oil seemed absurd. A strictly homemade diet would also require additional vitamins and minerals, and the idea of adding more pills to Hustler's daily count of seven was not an option I could stomach. I resolved that Hustler's new diet would require me to get more creative.

My recipe for doggy weight loss would not call for beakers, burners, tubes or flasks. I thought about crazy diets that involve insufferable brews and eliminating food groups, which contradict the nutritional basics we learn in grammar school. I've witnessed friends' weights fluctuate from improper diets that dictate radical short-term eating habits. Hustler's new diet required sensible long-term meal and treat formulations to prevent future weight gain or other adverse affects. I began with my primary enemy, the kibble.

How many calories are in your dog's commercial food?
- **Dry Food**: Write down how many calories are contained in a single cup of your dog's kibble. (1 cup = 8 oz)
- **Wet Food**: Write down how many calories are contained in each can or pouch of your dog's food.

I chose to reduce Hustler's kibble to half the manufacturer recommended daily serving for his weight goal. Instead of the recommended 3 cups (1,389 calories), he would receive 1½ cups (694.5 calories), approximately 60% of daily food intake based on an 1100 calorie diet, ensuring proper vitamin and nutrient intake.

RULE: If your dog is overweight reduce commercial food by 25% of the recommended food servings for your dog's ideal weight range, not his or her current weight range. Depending on how many pounds your pooch needs to lose, you can reduce food up to 50% *(see OBESE servings).*

If your dog is obese reduce commercial food by 50% of the recommended food servings of your dog's ideal weight range, not his or her current weight range.

What will be your dog's new commercial food serving?

✎ Remember weight ranges for breeds are often broad and independent of other factors, such as height and muscle tone. If you have a mixed breed it may be very difficult to identify his or her proper weight range. You should speak to your vet before deciding what is ideal for your dog.

NEW COMMERCIAL FOOD DAILY SERVINGS (DRY FOOD) CHART

If the commercial food recommended serving portion as printed on the label for your dog's ideal weight range reads:	If your dog is OVERWEIGHT (BCS 4), change to: (Your dog's new daily commercial food serving)	If your dog is OBESE (BCS 5), change to: (Your dog's new daily commercial food serving)
½ cup (4 ounces)	6 tbsps per day *approximately*	¼ cup per day
1 cup (8 ounces)	¾ cup per day	½ cup per day
2 cups (16 ounces)	1½ cups per day	1 cup per day
3 cups (24 ounces)	2 ¼ cups per day	1½ cups per day *Hustler's daily serving*
4 cups (32 ounces)	3 cups per day	2 cups per day
5 cups (40 ounces)	3 ¾ cups per day	2½ cups per day
6 cups (48 ounces)	4½ cups per day	3 cups per day

If you feed your dog commercial wet food, I suggest you follow the dry food conversion guidelines and reduce food servings by 25-50%. Hustler has always been fed two meals a day, a small one in the morning followed in the evening by a larger dinner portion. If you are only feeding your dog one meal per day, *change to it to two*. Imagine waking up and going the whole day with only snacks. You'd probably be hungry, eat more and even be a bit cranky. I certainly would not be fun to be around if I missed a morning meal. Skipping breakfast is never an option for me, nor will it be for my dog.

Your dog's new daily food serving must be divided to include two meals.

 Meals, with an *S!*

TWO MEALS CHART

New Daily Servings of Commercial Food	Breakfast = 1/3 of Daily Serving	Dinner = 2/3 of Daily Serving
1/4 cup (2 ounces)*	1 tablespoon *approximately*	3 tablespoons *approximately*
1/2 cup (4 ounces)**	2 1/2 tablespoons *approximately*	5 1/2 tablespoons *approximately*
3/4 cup (6 ounces)	1/4 cup	1/2 cup
1 cup (8 ounces)	1/3 cup	2/3 cup
1 1/2 cups (12 ounces) *Hustler's daily serving*	1/2 cup *Hustler's breakfast*	1 cup *Hustler's dinner*
2 1/2 cups (20 ounces)	1 cup	1 1/2 cups
3 cups (24 ounces)	1 cup	2 cups
3 1/2 cups (28 ounces)	1 1/4 cups	2 1/4 cups
4 cups (32 ounces)	1 1/4 cups	2 3/4 cups
4 1/2 cups (36 ounces)	1 1/2 cups	3 cups

* *(Measure 1/4 cup at start of day. Then take breakfast & dinner amounts from measurement.)*

** *(Measure 1/2 cup at start of day. Then take breakfast & dinner amounts from measurement.)*

Obviously our pups would never settle for just eating their new commercial food servings! I think Hustler would most likely pack a bag filled with stuffed toys, tennis balls and his Amazing Treat Machine and hit the streets if I dared attempt such a grievous act. Or he would lock me in the closet and raid the fridge. Can you imagine a Labrador settling for *only* 1 1/2 cups of food per day? Definitely *not* going to happen.

If I had only scaled back the kibble to the recommended amounts, Hustler would no longer be a *Sausage*, but he would still be a *Big Boy*. In reducing the serving by half, we had calorie wiggle room for treats, but was it enough? Although his premium biscuits were, quote-unquote, low-fat, I was beginning to suspect that those timeless doggy treats were the real villains.

6 Treat Jars

It's only a treat, *right?*

Wrong. Have you met a dog whose head doesn't tilt to the side when hearing the word *treat?* I haven't. Since the time he was eight weeks old, Hustler has always been food motivated. I have successfully used that motivation in his training and to reinforce manners and behavior with (you guessed it) treats!

How did he learn to *sit?* I held out a treat until his rump hit the floor. How did he learn the *down* command? I held a treat on the floor until his body followed his nose down. How did I get Hustler to stop tugging on his leash? On our walks, I gave him treats when he kept the leash loose.

I wasn't handing him treats throughout the day because he looked at me or gave an adorable wag. I'd ask him to *sit, lie down, give a shake, bow.* Even though Hustler's training was successful, I handed out treats as rewards for his continued good behavior. His obedience, kindness and loving nature are achievements reached, at least in part, *because* of treats.

Just say the word *treat*. Notice an inflection in your voice. You may even smile as the tip of your tongue taps the roof of your mouth. It's a fun word to say and, more importantly, for our dogs to hear.

Treat, treat, treat. Did you get your dog's attention?

I believe any dog accustomed to receiving rewards should still get them. If I had followed my vet's advice by eliminating treats, I am convinced Hustler would have become a different dog. His happiness would have been jeopardized, his gentle nature lost and, perhaps, he would have developed behavioral problems. I had already eliminated hiking, running and long walks from his life, which is heart-wrenching to do to a Labrador Retriever. He already made so many sacrifices. I refused to take away his treats, too.

Besides, eliminating treats reminded me of the outdated diet motto, *eat less and lose weight*. While following this trend may lead to rapid weight loss, it does very little to promote and maintain a healthy metabolism, meaning results are usually temporary. I know people and dogs have different digestive processes and metabolic rates, but they are not *that* different. And I know my own metabolism is faster because of regular, healthy snacking.

Hustler's metabolism slowed after being neutered and would continue to diminish with age. I surmised that a meals only diet would grind his metabolism to a halt, hurting his long-term health. Remember, additional exercise would never be an option for him. If I took the *eat less* approach, I could only combat future weight gain with more drastic cuts in serving sizes. *What if in two years he could only eat a single cup of kibble to avoid weight gain?* He might be thin, but he would definitely be miserable, longing for the days when his bowl was full and treats were plentiful.

Since I had been buying processed dog treats, I decided to actually read that label, too. Without identifying the manufacturer, I will disclose Hustler's treats were premium, made from natural ingredients, low in fat and contained 40 calories per treat. According to my 48-hour list, he ate 10-15 biscuits a day, which equaled an eatra 400-600 calories. Sure, I could have broken the biscuits to space out treat times and ration calories, and I'm certain it would help shed a few pounds. But Hustler was almost 30 lbs overweight. I needed to do better than split a few treats in half.

While researching my vet's advice online, Hustler lay asleep beside my chair. His snoring became snorting, as if layers of fat impaired his breathing. Then I recalled that obese dogs are at serious risk for respiratory diseases. My thoughts raced. I felt faint. I desperately needed a snack to regain energy.

Hustler followed me to the kitchen and waited while I prepared a fruit plate. He looked at me with sad eyes. I instinctively went for the treat jar. His ears perked at the turning of the metal lid. Then, it hit me. *Why feed him a dry biscuit while I eat an apple?* I had been so preoccupied with research that I neglected the canine perspective.

Do you think a small, dry biscuit would satisfy the need for a snack more than an entire apple? Neither does your dog. I stood there and questioned why I spent time reading and rereading all manner of doggy diets, when I have a strong understanding of healthy eating, and certainly Hustler's needs.

I had my answer. And I knew what to do.

7   Chopped Up

I love the holiday season. It's my favorite time of year, when colorful lights adorn homes and feelings of childhood nostalgia bubble up when Bing Crosby plays on the radio.

It was the day after Christmas. The stockings were down. The last remnants of wrapping paper dotted our tree, which still sparkled from the tinsel and ornaments. I was relaxing on the couch, when I noticed Hustler sniffing at the floor that previously held our presents, and in particular, one present he never received.

Seeing him search for the missing present reminded me of apples. Yes, apples, and how they compare with his usual treat, the dry biscuit. Apples are higher in sugar, as are many fruits. But they are also very low in saturated fat and sodium, cholesterol free, and high in dietary fiber and vitamin C. Apples are a natural, healthy option, and can be enjoyed longer than a couple of biscuits. Apples are also economical. And although they don't require a prescription, one a day will keep the vet away!

It was settled. Apples would be part of my equation. After subtracting 694 calories for kibble from an 1100 daily allotment, I essentially had 400 calories to work with, which is not a lot. It reminded me of my 700 square foot apartment in NYC. At first, the closets seemed impossibly small. But with some clever organization, I had room for all my shoes!

It was up to me to figure out what new treats to feed Hustler. So, I naturally thought of the foods I enjoy. If I like them Hustler will like them, too, *right?* Maybe. Since he's a Lab, I was optimistic he would eat just about anything. But before I could plan a grocery list, I needed to identify human foods that are toxic to dogs. We all know about the *no alcohol* rule. Yappy hours are dog friendly events at restaurants, not a time to serve doggy martinis.

All jokes aside, there are foods that can be very harmful to your dog. The different foods vary in toxicity and effects, including digestive problems, severe illness and sometimes death. Just avoid them and your dog will be fine. To help identify these harmful and potentially fatal foods, here's a list I compiled mainly from The American Society for the Prevention of Cruelty to Animals (ASPCA), and a few additional reputable online sources. You should also check with your vet to confirm if there are any other foods your pup should specifically avoid.

Human Foods Not To Feed Your Dog
- Alcohol/Ethanol (also known as ethyl alcohol, grain alcohol or drinking alcohol)
- Avocados
- Baby food
- Bones from fish, poultry, or other meat sources
- Caffeine in all forms, including coffee, tea, as well as grounds
- Chocolate
- Citrus oil extracts
- Cooked fish as it may contain bones – Canned cooked boneless fish is safe
- Fat trimmings
- Fresh or cooked hops
- Fruit seeds or pits

Human Foods Not To Feed Your Dog (cont'd)

- ◎ Grapes, raisins and currants
- ◎ Macadamia nuts
- ◎ Milk or other milk-based dairy foods
- ◎ Moldy or spoiled foods
- ◎ Mushrooms
- ◎ Nutmeg
- ◎ Onions, garlic, shallots, scallions and chives (raw, cooked or in powder form)
- ◎ Potato peelings, green potato parts and tomato plant leaves
- ◎ Raw eggs
- ◎ Raw fish
- ◎ Raw meat
- ◎ Rhubarb leaves
- ◎ Salt, baking soda and powder
- ◎ Sugary foods
- ◎ Table scraps
- ◎ Tobacco
- ◎ Xylitol and other artificial sweeteners
- ◎ Yeast dough or bread dough

See Appendix I for more detailed information, including medical conditions caused by these foods.

I was thinking about all the food Hustler should avoid when I watched him lie down on the tree skirt. He let out a loud sigh. I knew why. The day before, on Christmas morning, there was a gift for him on that spot. Every year, a close friend gives Hustler the same present: a box of gourmet holiday biscuits. I forgot about it, until I noticed him pawing at it. I jumped up and snatched the gift from his grasp.

Hustler looked at me, then at the box, then under the tree, then back at the box. It wasn't fair that frosted biscuits had become dangerous to his health. Since he recognized the box, I broke off a very small piece of biscuit before throwing the others away. His attention went back to a new squeaky toy, but before long, he walked over to the garbage and sat in protest.

It killed me to watch him sulk. But his treats needed to be healthy foods that would benefit his waistline. I ruled out specialty and exotic foods to buy week after week, which can be difficult to find and expensive. It made more sense to consider the foods I regularly ate.

Since I snack on apples, I decided to investigate fruits before exploring veggies. A word of caution: Beware of online posts, blogs, message boards, et cetera, in dog communities and forums where passionate owners chime in with pro- or anti-fruit commentary. Although everyone is trying to help, the discussions tend to be confusing and misleading, with many opinions masquerading as facts. I confirmed that many fruits are safe for dogs, based on ASPCA guidelines, as well as information from other reputable sources.

Fruits Safe To Feed Your Dog

All fruits must be washed, cleaned, and must not contain pits, seeds, stems, leaves or plant parts, as these are toxic. If the fruit contains skin you wouldn't eat, then peel.

Apples	Honeydews	Pears
Apricots	Mangos	Pineapples
Bananas	Melons	Plums
Blackberries	Nectarines	Raspberries
Blueberries	Oranges	Strawberries
Cantaloupes	Peaches	Watermelons

See Appendix II for complete list, including nutritional facts, calories per serving, and additional details.

Ok, so I like sweet fruit. Guilty. Although these fruits have a lot of sugar, they also have many good points, including:

- very low saturated fat
- no cholesterol
- low to very low sodium
- high to very high dietary fiber
- high niacin
- high to very high potassium
- high manganese
- high to very high in vitamins A, B6, C

When compared to biscuits, fruits offer much more nutritional value. Anything growing on a tree is usually healthier than what is in a box, bag, can, tin or any other packaging I forgot to mention. But since fruits are high in sugar, I knew they would be given to Hustler as *secondary* treats.

I kept many citrus fruits off the list. Grapefruits are extremely acidic and can irritate humans with sensitive stomachs, so I didn't think they would be a good fit for a dog diet. And since the idea of snacking on a lemon or lime isn't particularly appetizing, they are crossed off as well. I also avoided small seeded fruits, such as kiwis and cherries, and any fruits I do not enjoy eating, such as cranberries and huckleberries, which are safe when fed in small amounts.

As a woman with a sweet tooth, I started my list with sweet treats. That said, it was time to look into healthier treats, also known as vegetables. Now, I love vegetables, but it was not love at first sight. I wondered if Hustler would treat them as I had in my youth, and hide them under the rug.

Vegetables Safe To Feed Your Dog

All vegetables must be washed, cleaned, and must not contain inedible leafy ends or plant parts typically removed, as these are toxic. If the vegetable contains skin you wouldn't eat, then peel.

- Alfalfa
- Asparagus
- Baby Spinach
- Broccoli
- Brussels Sprouts
- Butternut Squash
- Cabbage
- Carrots
- Cauliflower
- Celery
- Cherry Red Tomatoes
- Cucumbers
- Green Beans
- Green Sweet Bell Peppers
- Iceberg Lettuce
- Kale
- Peas
- Potatoes
- Pumpkin (not pie filling)
- Red Sweet Bell Peppers
- Romaine Lettuce
- Spinach
- Sweet Potatoes
- Zucchini

See Appendix III for complete list, including nutritional facts, calories per serving, and additional details.

> **The ASPCA states:** "the only vegetables we recommend you avoid are onions, scallions and garlic." There are certain caveats, such as cleaning, de-seeding, de-pitting, and avoiding green plant of some, but when these steps are taken, the fruits and vegetables listed are safe for dogs.

With vegetables, Hustler could snack on treats all day, while ingesting substantially fewer calories. I told myself I simply needed to cut out biscuits, not treats. The ingrained concept that all dogs eat biscuits is wrong. I must admit, I fed Hustler biscuits for years. But, no more! Fruits and vegetables would replace biscuits as treats, and also find their way into his bowl at mealtimes.

There were few a things to consider before shopping:
- Which fruits will be fed more than others?
- Which vegetables will be fed more than others?
- Most importantly: Which fruits and vegetables do I commonly purchase?

Some fruits and vegetables are seasonal, meaning they'll be considerably more expensive when out of season. For instance, if I wanted to give Hustler strawberries, I wouldn't give him more than one per day. If I bought a carton just for him, then the uneaten berries would spoil within a week. My mom taught me to never waste food, so Hustler would only enjoy strawberries if I were purchasing them for myself.

All foods impact dogs' digestion differently. For example, many fruits are not good for a dog's stomach if fed in larger amounts. It's important to keep this in mind when introducing the new foods. Until you know which foods will regularly be on the menu (can take one to two months), keep an eye out for signs of gastrointestinal (GI) upset. Like humans, some dogs have food allergies, which could make them intolerant to some ingredients, such as corn. If you think your dog may have an allergy, consult your vet before adding new foods to his or her diet.

Of the fruits I like, I selected fruits that are inexpensive and relatively bland, as they could be served several times a day. I chose:

- Apples
- Bananas
- Pears

Applying the same reasoning, I determined the rest of my shopping list. Vegetables should be the *primary* snacks for your dog as they offer great nutritional values and are lower in sugar than many fruits. I chose:

- Carrots
- Celery
- Cucumbers
- Green Beans

If you prefer other fruits and vegetables in your fridge or freezer, you do not need to absolutely follow my grocery list. I made decisions based on my palate and what was suitable for Hustler. Feel free to make whatever changes you deem necessary, as long as they are in keeping with the spirit of this diet.

I had never fed Hustler vegetables prior to *The Amazing Treat Diet for Dogs*. After a few early attempts, which resulted in him ignoring the healthy treats, I gave up. If you have tried to feed your dog vegetables or fruits in the past and he or she didn't chow down, then don't worry. Within an afternoon, Hustler quickly realized they were his only options and came running when he heard me say *carrot*.

While researching fruits and vegetables, I learned apples, as well as other fruits and vegetables, may provide holistic allergy relief. In addition to leg problems, Hustler suffers from seasonal allergies. His eyes will redden, his ears become hot and red, and he sometimes breaks out in hives. To keep the hives at bay and reduce itchy soreness, he receives four low dose antihistamine pills a day. If his eyes seem itchy, then I add canned boneless salmon to his dinner. Within an hour or so, he stops rubbing his eyes. Over the course of this diet, he has grown to love salmon and it has thankfully prevented his face from swelling up like Rocky Balboa after a fight.

FOODS WITH POTENTIAL HOLISTIC HEALING PROPERTIES

Foods To Potentially Help Relieve Allergy Symptoms

- Apples
- Blueberries
- Blackberries
- Broccoli
- Brussels Sprouts
- Butternut Squash
- Cauliflower
- Green Sweet Bell Peppers
- Mangos
- Oranges
- Pineapples
- Raspberries
- Salmon & Salmon Oil
- Sweet Potatoes
- Tuna & Tuna Oil

Foods To Potentially Maintain Good Bone Growth & Stave Off Arthritis

- Apples
- Asparagus
- Broccoli
- Brussels Sprouts
- Butternut Squash
- Cabbage
- Carrots
- Celery
- Chicken
- Cottage Cheese
- Egg Yolks
- Liver
- Kale
- Oranges
- Pears
- Salmon
- Spinach
- Sweet Potatoes
- Tuna

Foods Considered To Potentially Aid In Digestion

- Alfalfa
- Apples
- Bananas
- Broccoli *
- Brussels Sprouts*
- Brown Rice *
- Carrots *
- Celery
- Chicken *
- Cottage Cheese
- Green Beans *
- Melons
- Pears
- Pumpkin (canned, not pie filling)

Steamed or boiled

Foods Considered To Contain Cancer-Preventing Properties

- Alfalfa
- Apricots
- Broccoli
- Brussels Sprouts
- Butternut Squash
- Cabbage
- Carrots
- Cauliflower
- Liver
- Mangos
- Potatoes
- Pumpkin (canned, not pie filling)
- Salmon
- Spinach
- Sweet Potatoes
- Tuna

Foods Considered To Benefit Eyes & Vision

- Broccoli
- Carrots

Foods Used To Help Stop Stool Eating (Coprophagia)

- Brussels Sprouts
- Cabbage
- Pineapple
- Pumpkin (canned, not pie filling)
- Spinach

See Appendix IV for more detailed information.

I have only witnessed the healing qualities of canned boneless salmon, sweet potatoes, tuna and apples. I found them very effective in adding shine to Hustler's coat, reducing inner ear irritation and relieving dry, itchy skin and eyes. If certain foods may potentially prevent cancer and eye diseases, why not incorporate them in your dog's diet? I've never heard of a biscuit that can help with allergies, have you?

> **NOTE:** Canned boneless salmon and canned tuna should not be fed more than 3 times per week.

It was New Year's Eve and I was ready to start Hustler on his new diet the following day, as our shared resolution. I grabbed my shopping list, gave Hustler a hug with promises of a speedy return and, with a giddy smile, went off to the store.

My first purchases included:

3 Apples	1 Small bunch of celery stalks
4 Bananas	1 Cucumber
1 Pear	1 Bag frozen green beans
1 Bag of carrots (large carrots)	3 Cans of pink salmon

Since I wasn't quite sure what foods Hustler would like, I didn't want to waste money with large purchases. Also, to be completely honest, I had my doubts whether this diet idea would even work. Many chat room comments include stories about how dogs don't eat vegetables. Hustler was never fed human food, aside from chicken and occasional cooked liver, so I wondered if he would even eat an apple.

That evening, we had a dinner party. I announced Hustler would be starting a new diet the next day. Our friends, also dog parents, expressed how they always wondered why Hustler's weight never concerned me. I explained the *Sausage* story. After laughter subsided, I confessed that I didn't realize how fat he had become. As the night went on, Hustler started limping and spirits weren't so high. He was so excited to be hosting a party that all his walking around with excess weight had taken its toll. At midnight, I told Hustler his life was going to change the next day. I crossed my fingers and hoped it would be a change for the better.

II A New Year

8   The First Breakfast

After a night toasting the New Year, we decided to sleep in and snuggle. Back then, Hustler didn't eagerly wake-up in the morning. When the alarm sounded, we followed the routine. We went outside to take care of business, then headed into the kitchen to begin breakfast. As usual, Hustler lounged by his bowl, completely unaware of my plan.

I scooped the new ½ cup measurement and wondered if he sensed the reduced serving as the falling kibble dinged against his stainless bowl. It was such a small amount of food. *Was I being too strict?* No. His bowl would be full, just not with kibble. My options were apples, bananas and pears.

Old breakfast = 1½ cups kibble
New breakfast = ½ cup kibble & 1 large banana

I chose bananas because they are comfortable on the stomach and satisfy hunger well. Bananas are also great sources of potassium, but high in calories (9" banana = 135 calories). It is a good morning fruit, as the calories can be burned off throughout the day, after satisfying an early appetite. It seemed like the perfect addition to breakfast kibble, but would Hustler agree?

He approached his bowl, inspecting its contents. He gave it a cautious sniff. I smiled as he lowered his snout to taste the grub. He was intrigued, but his curious expression melted into one of appreciation. There was something new, something unexpected in his bowl. He licked it clean. We did a little hip wiggling, never-do-in-public dance. Inspired by the 1920's Frank Silver and Irving Cohn song, my husband sang:

Yes! We have your bananas,
We have your bananas today!
Yes! We have your bananas,
Bananas, bananas, hooray!

All seemed perfect, until about 30-45 minutes later, when Hustler's eyes beamed that *I'm hungry* look. I knew it was going to happen sooner than usual and it will happen to you, too. Hustler was accustomed to eating roughly 600+ calories in the morning. On this morning, he only consumed about 350 calories, a considerable difference.

It was clear. Hustler wanted more food.

It was time to test out the treat element of *The Amazing Treat Diet for Dogs.* He already had a fruit, with positive results. I figured it was time to try a vegetable.

9 The First Carrot

An hour after his first new breakfast, Hustler clearly wanted more food. In the past, I would ask him to *sit, lay down, shake, roll over*, et cetera, for a treat. But rather than give a command, I just looked at him. Fifteen seconds later, he started doing every trick he knew to get a treat. It was actually pretty funny. Imagine a dog cycling through every trick he or she knows at a rapid pace, much like a cartoon played at double speed, and you'll understand what I saw. We were ready to put this diet to the test.

I grabbed a large carrot from the bagged bunch, cut off the tip and leafy tail ends, washed it thoroughly and gave a *down* command. After he was in a down position, I responded with *Good Boy*. He earned his treat. I handed him a carrot.

He held the carrot in his mouth for a second, before dropping it on the floor. No licks, no chews, no bites, no nibbles, no eating whatsoever. Instead, he stared at the orange object. His eyes looked up with perplexing disbelief as if I had given him a bar of soap.

Hustler stood, left the carrot behind and walked away. There was calmness about him as if he were in the early stages of plotting another strategy. He sat by the treat jar and just stared at me. No barks, no demands, just a long, calculated stare. *Be strong, be strong*, I told myself. That large carrot may have more calories than a single biscuit, but it contains more vitamins, and more importantly, will take him longer to chew it. From now on, carrots would be his treats, whether he liked it or not.

He could sense my unyielding determination and frantically repeated his tricks, over and over. Again, I offered the carrot, but he did not accept.

Woof.

It was low in tone, but nonetheless assertive. He wanted a biscuit and he wouldn't let the issue rest. I stood my ground and offered the carrot again. With a painfully defeated expression, Hustler left the kitchen to lay down in the living room. My worst fear had become a reality. He was sulking. Although he never experienced punishment, he was feeling as though he had done something bad.

I immediately went to give him affection and remind him he is a good boy. After a few belly rubs received with smiles and licks, I knew his happiness had been successfully restored. I asked him if he wanted a treat. He bolted for the jar. I stayed seated in the living room. Once he realized I wasn't en route to the kitchen, he returned and glared at the carrot in my hand.

You probably think he just caved in and took it from me. Alas, he did not. He snuggled up beside me, put his head down and pouted. Loud sighs persisted for about ten minutes. I felt as if someone were twisting my stomach in knots. It was brutally difficult to see Hustler pouting and rejecting his new treats.

In a desperate attempt to convince Hustler the mysterious orange thing was indeed food, I pretended to eat the carrot. Then it hit me, or rather hit my nasal passage. The carrot didn't smell like anything! He needed a good scent to get him chomping. The only way to release the carrot's fresh aroma was to peel it. I ran to the kitchen with high hopes that only a few peels stood in the way of Hustler snacking healthily. I called for him, asked him to *sit* and rewarded him with the peeled carrot.

Voila! As soon as he sniffed the carrot, it was in his mouth. It took about three minutes for him to gnaw it into a shredded mess and another two minutes to swallow the shaved pieces. He snacked for about five minutes and only ingested 25 calories! I don't even know how many biscuits he would need to devour for a non-stop five minute snack feast, but they definitely would have exceeded 25 calories. And he smiled as he ate. The carrot was a new taste surprise and brought an exciting crunchy sensation!

What I learned from Hustler that day was essential in all future meal and treat planning. You need to understand that your dog is trying to *tell* you something. Even disobedience is communication of some sort. It wasn't until I thought about the situation from his perspective did I understand *why* he wouldn't eat the carrot. I also discovered canine and human perspectives aren't that different. These days, Hustler is much less particular about unpeeled carrots, but I pick up the peeler because that's how *we* prefer them.

10 The First Afternoon

Once I unlocked the secret for getting Hustler to eat a carrot, I was confident the diet would work. Of course, I would wash, peel, de-pit, de-seed, de-stem, chop ends and remove leafy greens. New treats would replace those dry unsavory biscuits. Yet I couldn't be reckless with my selections. Since fruits are higher in sugar and can affect the digestive system more than vegetables, fruits would be afternoon snacks as opposed to evening treats. I didn't want Hustler pepped up on sugar or suffering from poopie pants at 10 pm.

I wasn't worried about counting calories. They balance themselves out. The daily 1100 calorie goal would never be exceeded. I had successfully calculated a formula for Hustler to *eat more often* and ingest fewer calories.

16 old treats (640 calories)	16 new treats (3 being full carrots) (152.5 calories)
	75 calories (3 carrots)
	57 calories (5 apple slices with skin)
	10 calories (1 pear slice skinless)
	6 calories (1 celery stalk = 5 separate treats)
	4.5 calories (2 cucumber slices with skin)

When I look at these numbers, I wonder why I didn't start feeding him fruits and veggies sooner. It's probably the same reason many people don't eat as healthily as they should. Fast foods, fast treats. Grab 'em from a jar and hand to your pup. It is much easier to purchase pre-prepared foods than to cook. Many people don't have the time to sit and dine on healthy foods, so the drive-up window becomes a convenient solution, which is why I created this diet to be remarkably easy.

Plenty of vegetables and some fruits can easily be grab 'n go snacks. Wash, clean, chop and refrigerate in airtight containers. Your dog's treats stay fresher longer and they're easy to grab. Besides, after a day, celery loses its crunch when not properly stored. No one enjoys eating soft celery, especially Hustler. Unfortunately, most fruit turns brown very quickly. These treats take a minute to prepare, but it's worth the time.

That afternoon, I decided to designate a specific cutting board to prepare Hustler's treats. Maybe he was just excited, but Hustler immediately became more alert to certain sounds, like the cutting board, fridge door opening, utensils and faucet. He'll now come running to the kitchen, holding a treat toy with a look that says *fill it up!* And I do, after he sits and I make sure there are no particles of old food stuck in ridges, growing bacteria.

When it was time to go on a walk, I would cut a few bite sized apple slices and wrap them in a napkin. Hustler still pulled his leash whenever he saw another dog, so I needed treats during walks to keep him in check. On our first walk of the diet, he spat out a few apple bites, probably because he was expecting a biscuit. He soon realized it was an apple slice or nothing. Dogs are very contextual, which is why a dog trained to sit on a carpet may not respond when on concrete. Hustler needed to adjust to his new treats on walks, and he did.

The only other treat Hustler refused (at first) was the cucumber. It made sense. It doesn't possess a strong, appealing scent, which, as Hustler reminded me as he stared at an unpeeled carrot, is important to dogs. He didn't seem interested in cucumber slices, but it was a low calorie bland vegetable, so I persisted.

I had to be crafty and figure out a way to get Hustler to swallow the cucumber before eliminating it as a treat. I remembered a night when my mother tried to force me to eat meatloaf because she said it was good for me. It tasted horrible (sorry, Mom). I wasn't going to force Hustler to eat something he considered disgusting, but I certainly wouldn't accept him rejecting a food he never tried, either. I filled one of his toys with veggies and snuck in a few cucumber bites. Once he tasted the cucumber, he licked his chops and wanted more.

If your dog consistently dismisses a particular fruit or vegetable, then mix it in with other treats. If your dog still chooses not to eat it, either cross it off the treat list or try it again later in the diet, when your dog has become accustomed to a wider range of food. *The Amazing Treat Diet for Dogs* is about happy, healthy eating, not unpleasant force feeding.

11 The First Dinner

Hustler was restless. When I grabbed his leash, he ran for the door. He still had the strength to get going, but could no longer control his momentum at full speed. He lost his balance and slid across the wood floor. Fortunately, he crashed into my legs instead of our flat screen television. I felt the tremendous force of Hustler's doggy mass. In this case, it was from 96 lbs of flab, not muscle. Even though my knees ached, it made me smile to see his adventurous spirit had returned.

Our walk presented an interesting role reversal. I limped along while Hustler, filled with energy, trotted alongside. We reached the corner, which Hustler knew was our usual turnaround point. I turned back toward our home. He stood still in protest. He wanted to keep going, but I knew his hips (and my knees) needed to rest. So, I said the first thing that came to mind.

Dinnertime?

Hustler's eyes widened, his ears raised, and he swung around. He galloped down the street as waves of fat flapped over his ribs. I held onto the leash for dear life. I couldn't believe his enthusiasm. Although Hustler had become a fat pup, this was the first time he was *excited* about dinner.

Sometimes I enjoy cooking, but like most of us, sometimes I'd rather order take-out. My goal was for Hustler to lose weight without having to become the Julia Childs of canine cuisine. There were already diets that offered overcomplicated recipes. Besides, I didn't want to rush a ton of new foods into his system, only to cause an upset stomach.

I selected green beans as Hustler's dinner vegetable. Green beans are typically accepted by the digestive system and blander than many other vegetables, including broccoli and cauliflower. Also, green beans are inexpensive if purchased frozen and steam in minutes when cooked in a microwave. I would like to stress all dinner vegetables should be cooked to ensure smooth digestion, especially for fast eaters, like Hustler.

His dinner was prepared in less than ten minutes. It was larger than his previous suppers and around half the calories. Hustler had never eaten a warm meal. As I stirred the yummy steamed green beans, he furiously licked his chops. The kibble green bean medley smelled appetizing, even to me.

Old dinner 2 ½ cups of kibble (1,157.5 calories)

New LARGER SERVING dinner (603 calories)

1 cup kibble (463 calories)
2 cups steamed green beans (80 calories)
1 can boneless pink salmon to holistically treat his seasonal allergies (60 calories)
½ cup water to blend flavors and slow eating

BONUS: Salmon holistically aided seasonal allergies, added shine to his coat, relieved dry skin and watery eyes.

When Hustler lowered his muzzle into the colorfully filled bowl, he winced and made a frightening sound he had never made. *Did the beans burn him? Was the salmon making his stomach turn? Did I hurt my boy?*

No!

He was ecstatic! His moan was followed by gum smacking chews. When he finally looked up, I could see his dinner bowl had been licked clean, just like breakfast. I was two for two! I was happy. Hustler was happy. And I was certain, in time, his joints would be happier.

How do you identify the correct dinner vegetable servings for your dog?

✎ There's a simple formula that is as easy to remember as it is to practice.

 RULE: The serving amount is based on a two (veggies)-to-one (commercial food) ratio. In Hustler's case, 2 cups of veggies for every 1 cup of kibble.

For example, if your dog receives…
- ¼ cup kibble, add ½ cup of vegetables
- ½ cup kibble, add 1 cup of vegetables
- ¾ cup kibble, add 1½ cups of vegetables
- 1 cup kibble, add 2 cups of vegetables
- 1¼ cups kibble, add 2½ cups of vegetables
- 1½ cups kibble, add 3 cups of vegetables
- 1¾ cups kibble, add 3½ cups of vegetables
- 2 cups kibble, add 4 cups of vegetables

My serving!

All you need to do is follow the two-to-one ratio for vegetable servings. Don't worry about exceeding the amounts by a few beans or sprouts, especially after an active day. Vegetables are a good source of vitamins and nutrients for your dog and very low in calories. Following your new commercial food servings is critical for success. But you can generously feed your dog

YUMMY MEAL TIP: Add cold water to soften dry food, blend flavors and slow down fast eaters.

vegetables, within reason, as long as you don't overfeed any single food. For instance, I know not to feed Hustler 4-5 cups of green beans at one sitting. Understand that any safe fruit or vegetable can be harmful if fed in excess. Just as it's unhealthy for a human to subsist on a green bean-only diet, it's not healthy for your dog, either.

There is one final ingredient Hustler receives in his bowl. He gets seven pills daily. In the past, I wrapped the pills in deli meat slices, which he had gladly gobbled up. But I wanted to eliminate processed meat from his diet. If your dog is fussy when it comes to taking meds, then stick with what works. However, if your dog is like Hustler and you are currently employing the meat wrap method, then try our approach of just throwing the pills in the bowl. With larger pills or vitamins, like Hustler's Glucosamine, break the pill in half so its size is comparable to a piece of kibble.

I remember looking at Hustler trying to sit by the doorway, shuffling to balance his weight on his back legs and ultimately slipping down. When I researched this diet, I never imagined my dog could lose 27 pounds in less than five months. But at that moment, I just wanted those rolls to disappear from his hips so the weight wouldn't keep him down.

Amazing Thin & Happy Lifestyle

12 Tough Love

I hope by now you have abandoned the myth that dogs don't eat vegetables. Most dogs would probably chose a fatty biscuit over a celery stalk at first, but in time they salivate at the word *celery*. Hustler comes running faster to the snap of a celery stalk than the squeak of his treat jar lid. It makes sense. Celery is larger in size, so he enjoys it longer, and crunching it is more fun.

However, not every new treat may be successfully received. You may have some obstacles the first day, as I did with Hustler and carrots. Your dog may not finish the green beans in the first night's dinner. Your dog may spit out apples and carrots, while you struggle to understand what you are doing wrong.

Allow me to be direct. Your dog is overweight, possibly obese, and at risk for very serious, potentially life threatening health problems. If your dog has limb issues, including arthritis, and is overweight, your dog is experiencing unnecessary pain.

We all know how our little furry tailed sweethearts can win us over with a glance or wag. Your dog is testing you to see if, by refusing the carrot, you will give in and grab the fatty biscuit. Do not give in! Your dog *can* survive hours without treats. You are not being cruel. It's called *tough love*, for you and your dog.

It's not that different from someone asking you to chose between a chocolate chip cookie and a carrot. Which would you chose? Now, imagine someone has fed you a cookie every day. Then, out of the blue, this person hands you a carrot. You'd probably ignore the carrot, waiting for the cookie. It's the same for your pup. Never underestimate your dog's intelligence and ability to read you. Your dog needs to know the cookie days are *over*.

Even a hard-to-please dog will happily accept healthy treats within a few days. By then, expect a *woof* for a carrot. Always remember that if your dog didn't love eating, you wouldn't be reading a canine diet book. Seal your biscuits, cookies and other doggy treats in an airtight container. They're not going to be around for a while!

13 The Second Day

It was morning. I was in bed, trying to get the energy to start my day. I was half-asleep, but I suddenly got the feeling that I was being watched. I opened my eyes.

Hustler lay at the foot of the bed, resting his head against his paw. As I slowly rolled out of bed, Hustler sprang up, and left the room. I grabbed my robe and followed after him. I turned the corner into the kitchen, where he patiently sat by his bowl.

I decided to continue feeding Hustler a banana each morning. He likes the taste and his pills mash well into the slices. For smaller breeds and dogs with ideal weight ranges below 35 lbs, I suggest serving only half of a banana. Other fruits can be substituted, after they are washed, peeled, and cleaned of pits, stems, and seeds, but we like bananas.

Hustler's Breakfast:
   1 banana mixed with ½ cup dry kibble

   "YUMMY!"

By that afternoon, Hustler's mood and energy level were noticeably different. He no longer slinked around the house, wasting the afternoon. He was always a happy dog, but I knew he was unsatisfied with a life spent mostly indoors. Dogs came over for visits, but play-dates needed constant supervision. At times, I thought I should let Hustler run with the pack. But running always led to limping, so I knew better.

However, Hustler always has a way of surprising me. There's a really funny thing he used to do when he got excited. We call it *the puppy shuffle butt*. It's hysterically bizarre and I hadn't seen him do it in over a year. His head spastically snaps from side-to-side as he flashes a maniacal grin. Crouched, with his back legs impossibly bent to his chest, he spontaneously gallops in a small, twisting circle, like a furry ballerina with motion sickness. I thought I would never see him do it again, but there he was, doing *the puppy shuffle butt*, a whirling picture of doggy exuberance. He wasn't as fast as I remembered, but he was finally becoming himself again.

I sincerely hope your dog never suffers from health conditions that cause you to restrict his or her activities. There's nothing harder than telling a dog to stop doing something because his or her body can't take it. If weight has physically prevented your pup from running or going on extended walks, just follow this diet and that won't be a problem much longer.

On our evening walk to the corner I discovered another recognizable physical reaction to his new diet. Luckily, I had an extra baggy. Without describing how beneficial vegetables are to the digestive system or embarrassing Hustler, I will say that after he started the diet, he typically has four bowel movements daily, normal in shape, size, texture and color. (Sorry Hustler, your business is important.)

14 The First Month

Hustler started greeting me at the door when I came home with groceries. He loved sniffing out the vegetable bags. We spent more time together in the kitchen, preparing snacks and creating fridge space for his new foods. The fruits and vegetables were providing a great source of vitamins and minerals, in addition to delicious tastes he clearly loved eating. I wasn't sure how much weight he was losing, but I knew it was at least *some*. He really did seem happier and more energetic. The diet was working!

I even started giving Hustler more treats! Most days, he would eat 15 snack size carrots, nine apple slices, 13 snack size bites of celery and a few pear slices. That's 40 treats!

> **RULE:** In addition to the morning banana and evening vegetables, always include at least three different snacks daily, to avoid consuming excessive unhealthy amounts of any one food.

As I'm sure you know, dogs are great listeners. I always talk to Hustler. When I ask him a question, I'll either get a lick, wag, paw, grunt, woof and, at times, an exit. Upon hearing *treats*, he would lick my face, paw at my arm, woof and run to the fridge. To ensure a smooth transition to new foods and prevent digestive issues, I re-examined our safe fruit and vegetable list.

I could have continued feeding Hustler the same foods I had on our first day. He liked them and they were safe. But he had spent years eating the same meal, which, after developing this diet, seemed boring by comparison. I wanted him to celebrate a variety of foods, as I do. So, instead of resting on my laurels, I charted a meal plan for the entire week and prepared treats.

✎ Treat Preparation

- Wash all vegetables and fruits
- Chop vegetables and fruits that do not turn brown (such as apples and pears)
- Store in airtight bags or containers
- The refrigerator is your new treat jar!

WEEK 1 DAILY FEEDING PLAN

Breakfast	new commercial food serving (dry or wet food) & peeled and sliced banana
	Hustler's serving: 1/2 cup kibble, 1 large sliced banana, 1/4 cup water
	For smaller breeds and dogs with ideal weight ranges below 35 lbs, I suggest serving only half of a banana.
Late morning / Early afternoon treats	apple slices, pear slices, carrots
Late afternoon snacks	cucumber slices, carrots
Dinner	new commercial food serving & cooked vegetable serving
	I recommend starting with green beans.
	Hustler's serving: 1 cup kibble, 2 cups steamed green beans, 1/2 cup water
Night treats	celery stalks, carrots
	note: avoid sugary snacks at night

TIP: For allergies: add pink boneless salmon in two to three dinners weekly.

✎ Remember Food Vegetable Ratio: two-to-one
½ cup commercial food (dry or wet) = 1 cup veggies
1 cup commercial food = 2 cups veggies
1½ cups commercial food = 3 cups veggies

TIP: While fresh vegetables are excellent, I recommend frozen vegetables. They are more economical, often pre-cut, can be stored longer, and cook faster and easier, using a microwave. Each cup of frozen vegetables takes approximately one minute & 30 seconds to cook in the microwave.

✎ Fast & Easy Dinner Preparation
- Cook vegetables until tender
- Cut vegetables into bite-sized pieces using knife, food scissors or food processor
- Add vegetables to kibble – Make sure veggies are not too hot
- Optional: Add water to slow down fast eaters
- Stir to cool and blend flavors

Bon appétit!

After a successful week, we were ready to try new foods!

For Week Two, Hustler enjoyed raw green beans as treats. To mix things up, I added steamed broccoli to Hustler's dinner. Since I add 2 cups of vegetables to his kibble for dinner, I introduce new veggies in ½ cup servings.

RULE: When you introduce new dinner vegetables, test in small amounts to determine if the new vegetable will be right for your dog's digestion: 25% of total vegetable serving.

WEEK 2 DAILY FEEDING PLAN

Breakfast	new commercial food serving (dry or wet food) & peeled and sliced banana
Late morning / Early afternoon treats	apple slices, pear slices *Try a new fruit or vegetable! I recommend a few raw green beans.*
Late afternoon snacks	cucumber slices, carrots
Dinner	new commercial food serving & cooked vegetables serving Hustler's serving: 1 cup kibble, 1½ cups steamed green beans, ½ cup steamed broccoli, ½ cup water *Try adding a new vegetable! I recommend broccoli.*
Night treats	celery, carrots

TIP: It's easy to add new vegetables! Just cook vegetables together – Same bowl, same cooking time.

Depending on what fruits and vegetables you buy, experiment in small bite size pieces. Just a chunk of zucchini or boiled, skinless potato adds variety.

- Restock the vegetable basics: frozen green beans, frozen broccoli, carrots, cucumber and maybe some raw green beans
- Restock the fruit basics: apples, pears and bananas

Even if your dog's digestion is showing no warning signs, I suggest you hold off from introducing a new fruit or vegetable during Week Three. You have plenty of time to try meal combinations, and your pooch is probably loving all the new treats. I know you're excited to expand your shopping list, but don't overdo it. Even *healthy* foods are best enjoyed in moderation.

RULE: Only introduce one new fruit or veggie per day! That way, if your dog gets an upset tummy, you'll have no problem identifying the culprit.

WEEK 3 DAILY FEEDING PLAN

Breakfast	new commercial food serving (dry or wet food) & peeled and sliced banana
Late morning / Early afternoon treats	apple slices, pear slices
Late afternoon snacks	cucumber slices, carrots, raw green beans
Dinner	new commercial food serving & cooked vegetables serving Hustler's serving: 1 cup kibble, 1$\frac{1}{2}$ cups steamed green beans, $\frac{1}{2}$ cup steamed broccoli, $\frac{1}{2}$ cup water
Night treats	celery, carrots, cucumber slices, raw green beans

After several weeks, it was finally time to add new foods. Since we started the diet, I found myself snacking on Hustler's treats and we both needed a change. As much as I wanted more fruits, it would be best for Hustler to try new vegetables.

My shopping list already included:
Fresh apples or pre-cut apple slices
Fresh carrots
Fresh cucumber
Fresh green beans
Fresh pear
Frozen broccoli
Frozen green beans
Canned salmon

So I added:
Fresh zucchini
Frozen broccoli
Frozen mixed vegetables including cauliflower, carrots, butternut squash (must not include onions, not a stir fry medley)

WEEK 4 DAILY FEEDING PLAN

Breakfast	new commercial food serving (dry or wet food) & peeled and sliced banana
Late morning / Early afternoon treats	apple slices, pear slices *Try a new fruit or vegetable! I recommend raw broccoli spears or zucchini slices.*
Late afternoon snacks	cucumber slices, carrots, raw green beans
Dinner	new commercial food serving & cooked vegetables serving Hustler's serving: 1 cup kibble, 1 cup steamed green beans, $\frac{1}{2}$ cup steamed broccoli, $\frac{1}{2}$ cup steamed mixed veggies, $\frac{1}{2}$ cup water *Try adding a new vegetable to the green beans, such as a vegetable medley with squash and cauliflower!*
Night treats	celery, carrots, raw green beans

After four weeks, I could tell Hustler's waistline appeared smaller. I considered taking him to our vet for an official weigh-in. But I dreaded the thought of seeing her and hearing a new nickname. *Sausage* was bad enough. Besides, I knew he was losing weight, which was all that mattered.

15 The Months Ahead

We had successfully completed our first month on the diet. After a few early hiccups, it was effortless. Best of all, Hustler was going through some fantastic changes. He had increased energy and attentiveness. When I opened the refrigerator, I had to be mindful not to close the door on a wagging tail. If I called for him to *come*, he came and was ready to *sit, stay, heel, lay down* and *speak* upon command. He also had a shiny coat, smooth skin, healthy digestion and a newfound enthusiasm to leave his pillow. And it was all thanks to *The Amazing Treat Diet for Dogs!*

As you try this diet, don't worry if you stray from the weekly meal plans. This diet is not about strict schedules. Hustler and I needed fun, flexible, easily adaptable guidelines to eat healthier foods so weight loss could be independent of exercise. I had properly calculated the diet guidelines. I knew how to healthily balance the new foods Hustler enjoyed and could adjust the plan on the fly. You may choose to continue feeding your dog all the new foods from the first month. That would be perfectly fine and healthy for your dog. But if you're like me, and want to keep exploring new food combinations and treat possibilities, always remember there are a few rules to keep in mind:

Clean all fruits and vegetables
- Always remove stems, seeds, pits and leafy ends

Must have daily nutritional variety
- At least three different types of vegetables or fruits per day, in addition to a breakfast banana and dinner vegetables serving

Maintain dinner commercial food and vegetables serving ratio
- Always a two-to-one ratio for vegetables and commercial food:
    1 cup kibble = add 2 cups of vegetables

Always introduce new dinner vegetables in small servings
- 25% of total vegetable serving

Only introduce one new fruit or vegetable within a 24–hour period
- Be kind to your dog's tummy

The diet quickly became a lifestyle. On hot afternoons, frozen celery stalks and carrots were delicious chew toys. I confidently wore a chef's hat and experimented with food textures. I mashed, chopped, sliced and diced, while Hustler eagerly licked his chops in anticipation of the next taste sensation. Though I typically included green beans in his dinner, there were always other vegetables and sometimes fruits in his bowl. If I was making baked potatoes, then I would throw in a few cubes. If I was cooking Brussels sprouts, he would enjoy some. We happily cooked, laughed and ate together as pounds came off.

16 The Weigh-in

Hustler's waistline had returned, but it wasn't until the first week of May 2010 that I found out how much weight he lost. He needed to receive a yearly immunization shot. I could no longer cowardly hide from the vet. I was curious to know exactly how much weight Hustler had lost. But I feared it wasn't enough. I had been giving him almost double the amount of treats and he was eating larger meals. *What if the diet wasn't that amazing?* There was only one way to be sure.

It was raining, which always feels weird in Los Angeles. We parked and both stared at the vet's office. I looked at him and asked, *Okay, boy, are we ready?* He let out a loud *woof*, which I took as meaning *yes*.

We checked in with the receptionist. She peaked at his file and sneered, *He needs to be weighed before you can see the vet*. I knew she was just following protocol, but I detected judgment in her voice. She plopped down the file, which had a red sticker on it. I wondered if red was code for *obese*.

I looked at Hustler. He sniffed the scale, then backed away, like he knew what the wrong number would mean. I hit the reset button. He hopped on. The scale creaked. I thought *oh no*.

The digital numbers flickered. He stood still. I held my breath. I think he did, too. The numbers slowed like a roulette wheel ticking to a stop. I closed my eyes and immediately heard a beep. I opened one eye, as if seeing the scale with both would have resulted in a higher number. Then, I gasped.

69 lbs.

I did a double take when I saw that number flash on the bright red LED display. I screamed *Hooray!* Hustler peered up at me, wagging his tail. The receptionist asked for the number. When I said *69*, she didn't believe me and had to look for herself. She looked at the scale, then at the file, then the scale, then back to the file. She shuffled papers, scanning his charts. She announced that there must have been a mistake in his file, since his last weigh-in registered 96 lbs.

My smile widened. I confirmed, *He did weigh 96 lbs, but now weighs 69 lbs.* The statement attracted the attention of other receptionists and patients, including a woman who sat by the doorway with a morbidly obese beagle, violently panting. Everyone asked *how* he lost so much weight so quickly. A friendly vet technician jokingly asked if I were starving him, since she had never witnessed such an extreme weight loss, then complimented his coat's shine and fullness.

As we walked to the exam room, I listened to the contagious whispering and watched as everyone stared at Hustler. Since our former vet was no longer at the office, we were greeted by a new veterinarian, who questioned his identity because she was expecting an obese Lab. When I confirmed Hustler once weighed 96, she asked, *How did you do it?* I immediately realized the uniqueness of his weight loss.

Unfortunately, our former vet had left the practice a week earlier. She never learned how *Sausage* had gone from 96 to 69 pounds in only four months.

On our way out, I spied the receptionist scraping Hustler's file with her nails. I didn't make the connection until we were on the road. She was removing that red sticker.

17 Turning the Corner

After seeing reactions to Hustler's dramatic weight loss, I realized what I had accomplished is rare. I conceived and formulated a healthy, manageable weight loss plan that prevented additional pain and potential diseases caused by obesity. Unlike most diets, I never needed to worry about feeding him too many treats. He was no longer a statistic. He was an extraordinary success story that I knew needed to be shared to save the lives of other dogs.

The months that followed brought happiness, and a few hardships. Even though Hustler no longer carried excess weight, his dysplastic hips and elbows still caused him pain and required surgeries. Since he now maintained a healthy weight, he was an ideal surgical candidate.

In the summer, Hustler had arthroscopic surgery on his front legs. He had a total hip replacement performed on his right hip and was fitted with a titanium implant to provide him one strong leg. The recovery time was three months and involved considerable bed rest, but I wasn't worried about weight gain. Hustler enjoyed the same number of treats and meals, only gaining three pounds while his hip tried to heal. Although surgical successes are often achieved when patients are thin and in ideal health, sometimes they fail due to uncontrollable variables. Weeks after I began writing this book, x-rays indicated Hustler's hip had rejected the implant. He needed a Femoral Head Ostectomy (FHO). It was a second major surgery within five months.

I cried, and even screamed *this isn't fair!* I thought of every worst case scenario, of every medical complication, of the risks of anesthesia, of a gleaming scalpel rising over Hustler as he drifted to sleep on the operating table. Then I thought of all the good times, of the fat pup we picked from the litter, of ocean swims, of the chilly mornings when he would climb into bed and curl up beside me.

I wanted to wait in the lobby so I could get the news as soon as he was out of surgery. But my husband convinced me it was better to wait at home and occupy ourselves with other things, to spare the emotional torment of knowing our Hustler was unconscious on the other side of the wall. I spent that afternoon in a daze, numb to everything happening around me. Hours passed. The house was so quiet. Then, the phone rang.

I leapt up and answered it. It was the surgeon. He didn't bother with the pleasantries. *He's fine.* I really don't remember the rest of the conversation. I heard everything I needed to hear.

Each day, Hustler reminds me that no matter what happens, we will always overcome any obstacles no matter how daunting they first appear. His hip will heal in time. Even if he needs a front wheeled chair, he will never stop being a dog again. In overcoming obesity, his life has been extended. He is my daily inspiration. Whenever I have to make a difficult decision, I look to him and think, *If I can help him to lose almost 30 lbs in four months, then anything is possible.*

For the first time in over a year, we were able to walk to the corner and not turn around. We walked another block, and then another. On the way back, we crossed the final crosswalk. Hustler led me the entire way, but he unexpectedly plopped down in the middle of the street. Every fear I had concerning his health resurfaced. *Did I walk him too far?* I hunched over to see if he was okay. Before I could touch him, he rolled on his back, stretched his body out on the warm asphalt, and flashed his winning smile. Relieved, I rubbed his tummy, told him he was a good boy, and handed him an apple slice. I didn't realize the light had changed and we were obstructing traffic. But instead of an angry honk, the car at the intersection wheeled around us. The driver stuck his head out and said, *That's a beautiful dog,* and drove off. Hustler basked in this small victory, chewing on his treat, then got up, and led us back home.

Thank you for reading our story. We wish you and your dogs long, happy, healthy lives.

Starting Your Dog on
The Amazing Treat Diet

18 Amazing Treat Diet Key Points

Here are the things you need to know about following *The Amazing Treat Diet For Dogs*. Always follow the rules and keep in mind the guidelines as you adapt this diet to fit your lifestyle and your dog's appetite.

Instructions:
1. Identify whether your dog is obese or overweight *(Body Scoring Chart, p. 20)*
2. Identify your dog's ideal weight range *(p. 29)*
3. Identify your dog's necessary daily caloric intake amounts *(p. 30)*
4. Identify daily commercial food recommended servings for your dog's ideal weight range *(p. 30)*

Then:
If your dog is OVERWEIGHT, reduce serving by 25%
If your dog is OBESE, reduce serving by 50%
(New Commercial Food Daily Servings Chart, p. 32)

Divide commercial food into breakfast and dinner portions:
Breakfast = 1/3 daily serving
Dinner = 2/3 daily serving
(Two Meals Chart, p. 33)

Breakfast: Feed new commercial serving amount *(p. 33)*
- Add 1 banana to commercial food if your dog's ideal weight is over 35 lbs
- Add ½ banana to commercial food if your dog's ideal weight is under 35 lbs

Fruit snacks: Identify safe fruit *(Fruits Safe To Feed Your Dog, p. 43)*
- *Always* wash & clean
- Remove *all* seeds, stems, pits, leaves and never feed molded, spoiled or unripe fruits
- Ideally feed in morning or early afternoon hours due to high sugar content
- Select bland fruits – To start, I suggest bananas, apples and pears

Vegetable snacks: Identify safe vegetables *(Vegetables Safe To Feed Your Dog, p. 44)*
- *Always* wash & clean
- Remove *all* seeds, stems, pits, leaves and never feed molded, spoiled or unripe vegetables
- Select bland vegetables – To start, I suggest steamed green beans (for dinners), celery, cucumbers and carrots (for snacks)

Dinner: Feed new serving amount *(p. 33)*
- Vegetable to Kibble ratio is two-to-one, i.e. 2 cups of vegetables for every 1 cup of commercial food *(Dinner Vegetable Servings, p. 64)*
- Recommended: purchase frozen vegetables, steam in microwave (approximate cooking time: one minute and 30 seconds per cup)
- Chop large vegetables to be size appropriate for your dog's mouth before adding to bowl

Fruits and Vegetables with Holistic Properties: *(Foods With Potential Holistic Healing Properties, p. 47)*
- Canned boneless salmon and sweet potatoes aid Hustler in seasonal allergy relief, improved his coat and reduced dry skin irritation

Digestion:
- Your dog's daily bowel movements will most likely increase by one or two – Bring extra bags on walks!

Temperament:
- Your dog may become much more enthusiastic at mealtime and increasingly attentive when he or she hears the refrigerator door open

RULES:
- Keep the two-to-one vegetable to commercial food ratio (p. 64)

- In addition to the morning banana and evening vegetables, always include at least three different snacks daily, to avoid consuming excessive unhealthy amounts of any one food (p. 72)

- When you introduce new vegetables at dinnertime, test in quarters to determine if the new vegetable will be right for your dog's digestion (p. 74)

- Only introduce one new fruit or vegetable per day (p. 75)

KEEP IN MIND:
- Always make sure to chop fruits and vegetables into bite-sized pieces proportionate to your dog's mouth and esophagus size. For smaller breeds and dogs that do not chew before swallowing, I suggest using a food processor.

- Raw vegetables are excellent when given in treat servings. Dinner vegetables, which are larger in serving, should always be cooked and chopped into small pieces to ensure complete nutrient absorption and smooth digestion. Dogs have a shorter digestive process and lack enzymes to properly break down raw vegetables, when fed in large amounts.

- Adding water to meals helps slow down fast eaters.

19 Transform Fruits & Vegetables into Grab 'n Go Snacks

After you go grocery food shopping, simply prepare the treats for the next few days. Clean, slice and store vegetables and fruits in airtight containers. It only takes about 15 minutes to clean and prepare your pup's new treats – always remove seeds, stems, pits, leaves, plant parts and inedible skins. Some fruits, such as pears and apples, cannot be sliced and stored, as they turn brown. I don't mind, though. When I give Hustler these treats, I enjoy a few, too. Now I snack less on cookies and more on fresh fruit. We've both lost pounds on this diet!

Apples
- Buy snack size (pre-cut, pre-cleaned and bite-sized). If you prefer to get whole apples and clean them, you cannot store sliced as they will brown and discolor. Would you eat a brown apple? No, and neither should your dog.

Carrots
- Buy snack size (pre-cut, pre-cleaned and bite-sized). This will be a primary snack so definitely stock up.
- Buy a few large ones. Peel, clean/chop off the leafy and butt ends. and wash. Great snack for chewers!

VEGETABLE AND FRUIT CONVERSION TREAT TABLE

Hustler regularly eats 35-40 treats per day, but that doesn't mean he eats 35 whole fruits or vegetables per day. Remember healthy foods become unhealthy when fed in excess, so chop and slice each single fruit and vegetable so your pup can enjoy many treats throughout the day!

FOR EXAMPLE, SOME APPROXIMATE RATIOS ARE:

1 large carrot chopped = 8 treats

1 large celery stalk chopped = 5 treats

1 cucumber chopped = 10 treats

1 apple chopped = 6 treats

1 pear chopped = 6 treats

Celery
- Store immediately. Will lose crunch very quickly if not stored in airtight container. Less crisp, less interest from your pup!
- Buy a bunch. Clean/chop off the leafy and butt ends. Then cut into 2-3" snack sizes.
- Keep 'em large. Clean/chop off the leafy and butt ends. Just like carrots, these make for great chewing snacks.

Pears
- Just like whole apples, prepare on demand.

20 The Hustler File

In experimenting with various fruits and vegetables, I discovered some are better as everyday treats, while others are best enjoyed as very small infrequent treats due to acidity. To help you plan your dog's new snacks, I have included what I refer to as *The Hustler File*.

FRUITS	VEGETABLES
	Raw or cooked, treats and dinner ingredients
Everyday fruits:	**Everyday veggies:**
Apples	Carrots
Bananas	Celery
	Broccoli
	Green Beans
Every few days fruits:	**Every few days veggies:**
Pears	Cauliflower
Peaches	Butternut Squash
	Cucumbers
	Spinach
	Sweet Potatoes
	Zucchini
Few bites every once in a while fruits:	**Few bites every once in a while veggies:**
Apricots	Asparagus
Blueberries	Baby Spinach Leaves

FRUITS	VEGETABLES
	Raw or cooked, treats and dinner ingredients
Few bites every once in a while fruits (cont'd):	**Few bites every once in a while veggies (cont'd):**
Cantaloupes	Corn (only in vegetable medleys – fed very small
Honeydews	servings)
Pineapples	Green Sweet Bell Peppers
Mangos	Iceberg Lettuce
Melons	Peas
Nectarines	Potatoes
Raspberries	Red Sweet Bell Peppers
Watermelons	Romaine Lettuce
Only a bite or two once in a while fruits:	**Only a bite or two once in a while veggies:**
Oranges	Tomatoes
Plums	
Strawberries	

Hustler's Favorite Food Combos

Since this diet is incredibly easy to adapt to fit Hustler's likes and what's in the fridge, I love creating fun new combinations.

Scratch-Free Salmon Supreme

1 cup kibble

½ can (3 ounces) boneless pink salmon

¾ cup steamed broccoli

¾ cup steamed green beans

½ cup boiled & mashed sweet potatoes

Chicken Woofdorf Stew

½ cup kibble (serving proportional to meat serving)

½ cup boiled well-done chicken (serving proportional to commercial food)

¼ cup brown rice

1 cup steamed green beans

1 cup steamed broccoli & cauliflower medley

Wags Special
1 cup kibble
$\frac{1}{2}$ cup boiled & mashed butternut squash
$\frac{1}{2}$ cup steamed carrots & peas
1 cup steamed green beans

Crispy Crunch Chow
1 cup kibble
$\frac{1}{2}$ can (3 ounces) boneless pink salmon
$\frac{1}{4}$ cup diced raw apple
$\frac{1}{4}$ cup diced raw celery
$1\frac{1}{2}$ cups steamed green beans

Vegetable Muttley
1 cup kibble
$1\frac{1}{2}$ cups steamed green beans
$\frac{1}{2}$ cup medley - steamed carrots, cauliflower & peas

Pooch Pot Luck
$\frac{1}{2}$ cup kibble
1 can (6 ounces) boneless pink salmon
$\frac{1}{2}$ cup boiled & mashed potato
$\frac{1}{2}$ cup steamed spinach
1 cup medley - steamed green beans & cauliflower

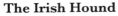

The Irish Hound
1 cup kibble
$\frac{1}{2}$ cup steamed Brussels sprouts
$\frac{1}{2}$ cup steamed cauliflower
1 cup boiled & mashed carrots

Summer Barks Delight

1 cup kibble
1 cup steamed green beans
½ cup steamed zucchini
½ cup seedless diced watermelon

If I add meat, such as well cooked boneless chicken or turkey, to Hustler's dinner, I always reduce his kibble serving by 25-50% depending on meat serving. I only reduce kibble serving by 25% when adding a full can (6 ounces) of salmon.

If I'm doing brunch, I'll substitute a scrambled egg or two egg whites with his breakfast banana.

OTHER FOODS SAFE FOR YOUR DOG (AND WHY HUSTLER DOESN'T EAT THEM)

I know many people feed their dogs these foods. I do not, and here's why:

- **Peanut butter:** It's high in saturated fat and I hate the smell, taste, and texture.

- **Bread:** I never thought it to be that nutritional for humans, let alone dogs.

- **Cream cheese:** It's high in saturated fat and I don't eat it.

- **Dairy cheese:** Although milk, cheese, and other dairy foods are not considered poisonous, unless spoiled or moldy, many dogs' digestive systems do not tolerate dairy foods very well. Hustler receives low-fat cottage cheese in small amounts to provide additional calcium and treat diarrhea, as instructed by our vet.

If Hustler didn't eat a food during his weight loss, there is no reason to include them as part of this diet.

21 Tummy Talk: What To Do When...

Digestion – Let it out!

Our dogs are our babies but their digestive tract is different than humans. Hustler never had digestive health issues, just the occasional *must have been something he licked at the park evening* bout of diarrhea. If your dog's digestion is healthy and bowel movements are clean and regular in color, size, and shape, you should be aware of how this most likely will change.

- Your dog will most likely increase his or her daily bowel movements, so bring extra baggies on your walks.

- You may occasionally notice small bits of undigested vegetables, like corn, well, in the poop, which is the reason Hustler only receives corn in small vegetable medley servings. I chop and cook all vegetables into bite-sized pieces proportional to Hustler's mouth and esophagus size. If you dog is a smaller breed, you may want to put the cooked vegetables into a food processor for a few spins.

It only took about four to five weeks to gauge how the fruits and vegetables affected Hustler's digestion. I found some vegetables, such as spinach and peas, when ingested in larger amounts, can cause flatulence, which is why you should only integrate different foods over time.

For example, if you wanted to try out spinach, broccoli, cauliflower, or perhaps a vegetable medley, introduce new vegetables in quartered servings *(see page 74 for additional information)*. Your pooch is about to have a radical change in his or her diet and you want a smooth transition, both in and out!

Poopie Pants

I've never known a dog that *never* had a little upset tummy. When this happens, the best thing to do is stop giving treats for a short time to let your dog's stomach recover from whatever turned it around. Each dog is different and some recover very quickly. You must use your judgment for feedings to allow time for your dog's gastrointestinal tract to simmer, which requires an easy transition with food.

I've outlined a few scenarios along with the meal servings that work for Hustler when he gets, what I call, *poopie pants*.

Mild, soft stools:

When Hustler's stool is soft but not loose:

Breakfast: still serve banana

Snacks: eliminate fruit and only give a couple of bite-sized carrot treats

Dinner: ½ to 1 cup of brown or white rice to kibble and reduce vegetable serving in half. You can substitute rice with boiled and mashed skinless potato.

When Hustler's stool is very soft but not liquid:

Breakfast: still serve banana

Snacks: eliminate snacks that morning and afternoon

Dinner: ½ to 1 cup of brown rice with skinless unseasoned well-cooked boiled chicken. You can add small serving of cottage cheese.

Runny, liquid stools:
- Stop feeding for approximately 10-12 hours.
- Give ½ cup serving of brown rice approximately every hour as long as Hustler is not experiencing diarrhea.
- After his stomach seems rested, I feed him a cooked egg, or skinless unseasoned well-cooked boiled chicken, and more brown rice.
- After 72 hours Hustler's stool is usually soft or mushy but intact, so I feed him according to those guidelines for a couple of days until his stool is normal in shape, size, and color.

In treating diarrhea, the ASPCA recommends "you avoid giving your dog any food for 12-24 hours while he's experiencing diarrhea, but do provide plenty of fresh, clean water to stave off dehydration." Additionally, be aware if any blood or mucus is present in the poop, or if it is black in color. If these conditions occur, if symptoms persist, or new symptoms become present, such as vomiting, lethargy, dehydrations or fever, contact your vet immediately. It's always safer to call your vet and learn your dog is fine than to wait and worry.

Constipation

Hustler has never had any issues with constipation. In fact, the diet's vegetable and fruit servings have given him a healthier digestion with more frequent bowel movements. You probably know what is regular and not regular for your best friend. You're the one holding the bag, right? But know that anytime you change your dog's diet there is a chance of irritating the regular flow of *business*. According to the ASPCA, if your dog has not done his or her business in over two days, strains, crouches or cries out when attempting to go, see your veterinarian immediately.

> "IF YOUR PUP ISN'T POOPING, CALL THE VET!"

Vomiting

It's always upsetting when your dog vomits. It usually happens because he or she has eaten something disagreeable or gobbled down too much food, too fast. If your chow hound chows down too fast then vomits, try adding water to the bowl to slow eating. Hustler is more excited to eat his meals now, so I add water to the bowl and find it does noticeably slow down his eating. In some situations vomiting can also be a sign of a more serious health issues. If your dog vomits more than once or if vomiting continues past one day, contact your vet.

✚ CALL YOUR VET IF...

There is always the possibility your dog's digestion can be negatively affected by a change in diet or have a reaction to a new commercial food. If your dog experiences any of the following reactions to *The Amazing Treat Diet for Dogs,* you should contact your vet immediately:

+ Shortness of breath
+ Rapid heartbeat
+ Weakness
+ Constipation – difficult, infrequent or absent bowel movements, which is one of the most common health problems associated with a dog's digestive system
+ Diarrhea - occurs more than two to three times in one hour, continues for more than a day, contains blood, or is dark-colored (black stool)
+ Vomiting
+ Unsuccessful attempts to belch or vomit
+ Retching without producing anything
+ Excessive salivation
+ Unnatural shedding
+ Skin reactions
+ Any unusual behavior your dog exhibits or abnormal physical changes

Appendix

Appendix I

HUMAN FOODS TOXIC FOR DOGS CHART

This chart is compiled based on dog health data published primarily by the ASPCA. The information is generally standardized but may vary based on source.

What to avoid:		Why to avoid it!
Alcohol / Ethanol also known as ethyl alcohol, grain alcohol or drinking alcohol		Even ingesting a small amount of a product containing alcohol may cause significant intoxication. In severe cases, coma, seizures and death may occur.
Avocados leaves, fruit, seeds and bark		Contain persin, an oil-soluble toxin, which typically only causes diarrhea and vomiting. In some animals, damage to heart muscle cells may occur, leading to heart failure.
Baby Food		May contain onion powder, which may be toxic to dogs.

What to avoid:		Why to avoid it!
Bones from fish, poultry or other meat sources		Dogs may choke or sustain a critical injury if bone splinters and becomes lodged in or punctures digestive tract.
Caffeine in all forms, including coffee, tea, as well as grounds		Depending on dose may produce the same toxic and potentially fatal effects as chocolate (see Chocolate toxicity for additional information).
Chocolate		Toxic compounds are caffeine and theobromine, which belong to a group of chemicals called methylxanthines. Darker chocolates are more dangerous, however all chocolates should be avoided.
Citrus Oil Extracts		Contains limonene and linalool (citrus oils with insecticidal properties), which are metabolized in the liver and may result in liver damage or failure.
Cooked Fish		Salmon & other fish COOKED: Because of small bones I choose to steer clear of fresh cooked salmon and other fish. Canned boneless fish is safe.
Fat Trimmings		Opinion: You've trimmed the fat because you chose not to eat it, so don't give it to your dog.
Fresh or Cooked Hops		Cultivated hops used for brewing beer have been associated with potentially life-threatening signs in dogs who have ingested them.

What to avoid:

Why to avoid it!

Fruit Seeds or Pits

Fruit seeds and pits may contain cyanide, particularly in the process of wilting. Signs of poisoning include: brick red mucous membranes, dilated pupils, difficulty breathing panting and shock.

Grapes, Raisins & Currants

Grapes and raisins are associated with development of kidney failure. Until toxicity is better identified, avoid feeding grapes or raisins to your dog.

Macadamia Nuts

Digesting macadamia nuts is unlikely to be fatal, but may cause very uncomfortable symptoms that may persist for up to 48 hours.

Milk or Other Milk-Based Dairy Foods

Dogs do not possess significant amounts of lactase (enzyme that breaks down lactose in milk). Milk and other milk-based products may cause diarrhea or other digestive upset.

Moldy or Spoiled Foods

Molds grow on food and some produce toxins, which may cause serious or even life-threatening problems if ingested.

Mushrooms

Certain wild species may be very toxic and known to cause liver and kidney damage, severe gastrointestinal and neurological effects.

Nutmeg

Nutmeg (Myristica fragrans) produces volatile oil, which may cause psychological effects. In large amounts, may cause vomiting, abdominal pain, seizures, as well as central nervous system excitation.

What to avoid:		Why to avoid it!

Onions, Garlic, Shallots, Scallions & Chives
raw, cooked or powder

Contain compounds that damage red blood cells ingested in sufficient quantities. While it's uncommon for dogs to eat enough raw onions and garlic to cause serious problems, exposure to concentrated forms, such as dehydrated onions, onion soup mix or garlic powder, may put them at risk.

Potato Peelings, Green Potatoes & Tomato Plant Parts
Solanum species

Ripe tubers are not considered toxic, but green parts contain solanine and other toxic alkaloids, which in large enough amounts may produce drooling, severe gastrointestinal upset, including vomiting and diarrhea, loss of appetite, drowsiness, central nervous system depression, confusion, behavioral changes, weakness, dilated pupils and slowed heart rate.

Raw Eggs

Raw eggs may contain potentially harmful bacteria, such as Salmonella and E. coli. Raw eggs contain avidin, an anti-vitamin that interferes with the metabolism of fats, glucose, amino acids and energy, and decreases absorption of biotin (a B vitamin), which may lead to skin and coat problems.

Raw Fish

Dogs fed raw fish or meat exclusively or in high amounts may result in a thiamine (a B vitamin) deficiency, leading to loss of appetite, seizures, and, in severe cases, death. Feeding raw salmon puts your dog at risk for Salmon Poisoning Disease (salmon infected with parasite called nanophyetus salmincola).

Raw Meat

Raw meat may contain potentially harmful bacteria, such as Salmonella and E. coli.

What to avoid:		Why to avoid it!
Rhubarb Leaves		Contains soluble calcium oxalates, which may cause kidney failure, tremors and salivation in dogs.
Salt, Baking Soda & Baking Powder		Large amounts of salt may produce excessive thirst and urination, or even sodium ion poisoning.
Sugary Foods		May lead to obesity, dental problems and possibly diabetes mellitus.
Table Scraps		Table scraps are not nutritionally balanced.
Tobacco		Nicotine found in cigarettes and tobacco products is highly toxic. Exposure to secondhand smoke may result in harmful inflammatory changes in airways and lungs.
Xylitol and other artificial sweeteners		Xylitol is a non-caloric sweetener that may lead to a rapid severe drop in blood sugar levels, disorientation and seizures. In large amounts, xylitol may cause liver failure, which may be fatal.
Yeast Dough or Bread Dough		Raw bread dough made with live yeast may be very hazardous.

Appendix II
FRUIT NUTRITIONAL CHART

This chart is compiled based on human and dog nutritional data. The vitamin and mineral contents are standardized but caloric content may vary based on source. All fruits must be washed, cleaned, and must not contain pits, seeds, stems, leaves or plant parts, as these may be toxic. If the fruit contains skin you wouldn't eat, then peel.

Apples

Flesh and skin of ripe apples is safe.

The steams, leaves and seeds contain substances known as cyanogenic glycosides, which are toxic. Apples are high in pectin, which is a gel forming fiber and may improve the intestinal muscle's ability to push waste through. Pectin also helps find and eliminate toxins.

Several human nutrition articles cite apples as containing omega-3s and omega-6s, which are known to relieve allergy symptoms.

Apples (cont'd)

1 cup (110 grams) = 57 calories

NUTRIENT	NONE	VERY LOW	LOW	HIGH	VERY HIGH
saturated fat		🥕			
cholesterol	🥕				
sodium		🥕			
dietary fiber				🥕	
vitamin C				🥕	
sugar					🥕

Good pectin source

Apricots

Flesh and skin of ripe seedless apricots is safe.

However, stems, leaves, pits and seeds are not safe for your dog to eat.

1 cup (165.0 grams) = 79 calories

NUTRIENT	NONE	VERY LOW	LOW	HIGH	VERY HIGH
saturated fat		🥕			
cholesterol	🥕				
sodium		🥕			
dietary fiber				🥕	
potassium				🥕	
vitamin A					🥕
vitamin C					🥕
sugar					🥕

Bananas

Peeled bananas are safe.

1 cup (150.0 grams) = 134 calories

NUTRIENT	NONE	VERY LOW	LOW	HIGH	VERY HIGH
saturated fat		🥕			
cholesterol	🥕				
sodium		🥕			
dietary fiber				🥕	
potassium				🥕	
vitamin B6					🥕
vitamin C				🥕	
sugar					🥕

Blackberries

Blackberries are safe.

1 cup = (144.0 grams) = 62 calories

NUTRIENT	NONE	VERY LOW	LOW	HIGH	VERY HIGH
saturated fat		🥕			
cholesterol	🥕				
sodium		🥕			
dietary fiber					🥕
magnesium				🥕	
manganese					🥕
potassium				🥕	
vitamin C					🥕
sugar					🥕

Contain free radical fighting antioxidants

Blueberries

 Blueberries are safe.

1 cup (145.0 grams) = 83 calories

NUTRIENT	NONE	VERY LOW	LOW	HIGH	VERY HIGH
saturated fat		🥕			
cholesterol	🥕				
sodium		🥕			
dietary fiber				🥕	
manganese				🥕	
vitamin C					🥕
sugar					🥕

Contain free radical fighting antioxidants

Cantaloupes & Melons

 Seedless cantaloupe and melon flesh is safe.

No data that melons or cantaloupe have the potential to produce effects beyond minor gastrointestinal irritation in dogs. These fruits are considered non-toxic. However, if any signs of gastrointestinal irritation occur, such as loss of appetite, drooling, vomiting or diarrhea, contact your veterinarian.

Some dogs love melons, but do not feed rinds as they have no nutritional value and are very unappetizing.

Cantaloupes & Melons (cont'd)

1 cup (156.0 grams) = 53 calories

NUTRIENT	NONE	VERY LOW	LOW	HIGH	VERY HIGH
saturated fat			🥕		
cholesterol	🥕				
sodium			🥕		
dietary fiber				🥕	
niacin				🥕	
potassium					🥕
vitamin A					🥕
vitamin B6				🥕	
vitamin C					🥕
sugar					🥕

Honeydew

Seedless honeydew flesh is safe.

As with all fruits, the seeds may contain cyanide. Do not feed rinds, as they are unpalatable and provide no nutritional benefit.

1 cup (170.0 grams) = 61 calories

NUTRIENT	NONE	VERY LOW	LOW	HIGH	VERY HIGH
saturated fat		🥕			
cholesterol	🥕				
sodium			🥕		
potassium				🥕	
vitamin B6				🥕	
vitamin C					🥕
sugar					🥕

Mangos

Seedless mango flesh is safe.

As with all fruits, stems, leaves, pits and seeds may be poisonous, and must always be removed. Since the skin may be thick and bitter in taste, peel before slicing.

1 cup (165.0 grams) = 107 calories

NUTRIENT	NONE	VERY LOW	LOW	HIGH	VERY HIGH
saturated fat		🥕			
cholesterol	🥕				
sodium		🥕			
dietary fiber				🥕	
vitamin A					🥕
vitamin B6				🥕	
vitamin C					🥕
sugar					🥕

Nectarines

Flesh and skin of ripe seedless nectarines is safe.

However, pits and seeds must be removed.

1 cup (138.0 grams) = 61 calories

NUTRIENT	NONE	VERY LOW	LOW	HIGH	VERY HIGH
saturated fat		🥕			
cholesterol	🥕				
sodium	🥕				
dietary fiber				🥕	

Nectarines (cont'd)

NUTRIENT	NONE	VERY LOW	LOW	HIGH	VERY HIGH
niacin					
potassium					
vitamin A					
vitamin C					
sugar					

Oranges

Seedless orange flesh is safe.

Stems, leaves, peels, fruit and seeds of citrus plants contain varying amounts of citric acid, limonin and oils, which may cause irritation and possibly even central nervous system (CNS) depression if they are ingested in significant amounts. However, a bite or two every so often is safe.

Oranges strengthen the immune system but should only be given in small amounts due to acidity.

1 cup (180.0 grams) = 85 calories

NUTRIENT	NONE	VERY LOW	LOW	HIGH	VERY HIGH
saturated fat					
cholesterol					
sodium					
dietary fiber					
potassium					
thiamin					
vitamin C					
sugar					

Peaches

Flesh and skin of ripe seedless peaches is safe.

Like all fruits, the seeds may contain cyanide and must never be eaten. Always remove stems and leaves as the plant itself is toxic.

Peach pits may obstruct digestive system when swallowed, which is why peaches are sometimes considered unsafe for dogs.

1 cup (170.0 grams) = 66 calories

NUTRIENT	NONE	VERY LOW	LOW	HIGH	VERY HIGH
saturated fat		🥕			
cholesterol	🥕				
sodium	🥕				
dietary fiber				🥕	
niacin				🥕	
potassium				🥕	
vitamin A				🥕	
vitamin C					🥕
sugar					🥕

Pears

Flesh and skin of ripe seedless pears is safe.

Like all fruits, the seeds may contain cyanide and must never be fed to dogs. Pears are a good source of water soluble fiber and help tone the intestines.

Pears (cont'd)

1 cup (165.0 grams) = 96 calories

NUTRIENT	NONE	VERY LOW	LOW	HIGH	VERY HIGH
saturated fat		🥕			
cholesterol	🥕				
sodium		🥕			
dietary fiber					🥕
vitamin C				🥕	
sugar					🥕

Pineapples

Pineapple flesh is safe.

Always remove leafy stems, and outer skin before serving. Feeding a teaspoon or two of pineapple flesh is a common homeopathic remedy to help stop stool eating.

1 cup (155.0 grams) = 78 calories

NUTRIENT	NONE	VERY LOW	LOW	HIGH	VERY HIGH
saturated fat		🥕			
cholesterol	🥕				
sodium		🥕			
dietary fiber				🥕	
manganese					🥕
thiamin				🥕	
vitamin B6				🥕	
vitamin C					🥕
sugar					🥕

Plums

Flesh and skin of ripe seedless plums is safe.

Stems, leaves, pits and seeds, which may be toxic, must be removed.

1 cup (165.0 grams) = 76 calories

NUTRIENT	NONE	VERY LOW	LOW	HIGH	VERY HIGH
saturated fat		🥕			
cholesterol	🥕				
sodium	🥕				
dietary fiber				🥕	
vitamin A				🥕	
vitamin C					🥕
sugar					🥕

Raspberries

Raspberries are safe.

Raspberries are good sources of quercetin, an antioxidant that diminishes the release of histamines, which minimizes allergic reactions.

Some research suggests that regular consumption of raspberries may be used holistically for those suffering from inflammation and pain.

1 cup (123.0 grams) = 64 calories

NUTRIENT	NONE	VERY LOW	LOW	HIGH	VERY HIGH
saturated fat		🥕			
cholesterol	🥕				

Raspberries (cont'd)

NUTRIENT	NONE	VERY LOW	LOW	HIGH	VERY HIGH
sodium		🥕			
dietary fiber					🥕
magnesium				🥕	
manganese					🥕
vitamin C					🥕
sugar					🥕

Contain free radical fighting antioxidants

Strawberries

Strawberries are safe.

Always remove all potentially toxic leafy tops.

1 cup (166.0 grams) = 53 calories

NUTRIENT	NONE	VERY LOW	LOW	HIGH	VERY HIGH
saturated fat		🥕			
cholesterol	🥕				
sodium		🥕			
dietary fiber					🥕
manganese					🥕
potassium				🥕	
vitamin C					🥕
sugar					🥕

Contain free radical fighting antioxidants

Watermelons

 Seedless watermelon flesh is safe.

Seeds and rind may cause gastrointestinal irritation.

1 cup (152.0 grams) = 46 calories

NUTRIENT	NONE	VERY LOW	LOW	HIGH	VERY HIGH
saturated fat		🥕			
cholesterol	🥕				
sodium		🥕			
potassium				🥕	
vitamin A					🥕
vitamin C					🥕
sugar					🥕

Appendix III
VEGETABLE NUTRITIONAL CHART

This chart is compiled based on human and dog nutritional data. The vitamin and mineral contents are standardized but caloric content may vary based on source. All vegetables must be washed, cleaned of any inedible leafy or hard ends and plant parts. If the vegetable contains skin you wouldn't eat, then peel.

Raw vegetables are great treats. Dinner vegetables should always be cooked until tender to ensure proper nutrient absorption and provide easy digestion.

Alfalfa Sprouts – Raw

Alfalfa sprouts are safe.

They are an excellent source of antioxidants.

1 cup (85.0 grams) = 25 calories

NUTRIENT	NONE	VERY LOW	LOW	HIGH	VERY HIGH
sodium			🥕		
calcium					🥕

Alfalfa Sprouts – Raw (cont'd)

NUTRIENT	NONE	VERY LOW	LOW	HIGH	VERY HIGH
vitamin A					
vitamin C					

Asparagus – Raw

Asparagus is safe.

Rich in many vitamins and minerals, asparagus is also a great source of vitamin K.

1 cup (134.0 grams) = 27 calories

NUTRIENT	NONE	VERY LOW	LOW	HIGH	VERY HIGH
saturated fat					
cholesterol					
sodium					
calcium					
dietary fiber					
iron					
magnesium					
manganese					
niacin					
pantothenic acid					
phosphorus					
potassium					
riboflavin					
selenium					
thiamin					
vitamin A					

Asparagus – Raw (cont'd)

NUTRIENT	NONE	VERY LOW	LOW	HIGH	VERY HIGH
vitamin B6					
vitamin C					
zinc					
sugar					

Good folic acid source

Asparagus – Fresh/Frozen, Steamed/Cooked/Boiled

1 cup (180.0 grams) = 40 calories

NUTRIENT	NONE	VERY LOW	LOW	HIGH	VERY HIGH
saturated fat					
cholesterol					
calcium					
dietary fiber					
iron					
magnesium					
manganese					
niacin					
phosphorus					
potassium					
riboflavin					
selenium					
thiamin					
vitamin A					
vitamin B6					
vitamin C					
zinc					
sugar					

Baby Spinach – Raw

Baby spinach is safe.

Since other vegetables are better sources of vitamins and minerals, chopped baby spinach leaves are primarily used to garnish Hustler's holiday meals.

1 cup (40.5 grams) = 13 calories

NUTRIENT	NONE	VERY LOW	LOW	HIGH	VERY HIGH
saturated fat	🥕				
cholesterol	🥕				
sodium				🥕	
calcium					🥕
dietary fiber				🥕	
iron					🥕
vitamin A					🥕
vitamin C					🥕
sugar	🥕				

Broccoli – Raw

Broccoli is safe.

This vegetable is rich in vitamins, contains cancer-fighting phytochemicals and anti-aging compounds essential to a balanced diet. Adding small, lightly steamed portions of this veggie to your dog's food promotes overall stomach and bladder health.

Broccoli is not a commonly reported poison, however may be toxic if fed in large amounts. Broccoli contains isothiocyanate, a powerful

Broccoli – Raw (cont'd)

gastrointestinal irritant and may be very painful. Broccoli in small amounts, less than 5% of a dog's diet, is nutritional as the bioflavonoid it contains potentially prevents cancer.

1 cup (88.0 grams) = 30 calories

NUTRIENT	NONE	VERY LOW	LOW	HIGH	VERY HIGH
saturated fat		🥕			
cholesterol	🥕				
calcium				🥕	
dietary fiber					🥕
iron				🥕	
magnesium				🥕	
manganese					🥕
pantothenic acid				🥕	
phosphorus				🥕	
potassium					🥕
riboflavin				🥕	
selenium				🥕	
thiamin				🥕	
vitamin A					🥕
vitamin B6					🥕
vitamin C					🥕
sugar				🥕	

Good folic acid source

Broccoli – Fresh / Frozen, Steamed / Cooked / Boiled

1 cup (87.0 grams) = 24 calories

NUTRIENT	NONE	VERY LOW	LOW	HIGH	VERY HIGH
saturated fat		🥕			
cholesterol	🥕				
sodium			🥕		
calcium				🥕	
dietary fiber					🥕
iron				🥕	
magnesium				🥕	
manganese					🥕
phosphorus				🥕	
potassium				🥕	
riboflavin				🥕	
thiamin				🥕	
vitamin A					🥕
vitamin B6					🥕
vitamin C					🥕
sugar				🥕	

Brussels Sprouts – Raw

Brussels sprouts are safe.

They are rich in antioxidants and natural antihistamines.

Brussels Sprouts – Raw (cont'd)

1 cup (88.0 grams) = 38 calories

NUTRIENT	NONE	VERY LOW	LOW	HIGH	VERY HIGH
saturated fat		🥕			
cholesterol	🥕				
dietary fiber					🥕
iron				🥕	
magnesium				🥕	
manganese					🥕
phosphorus				🥕	
potassium					🥕
riboflavin				🥕	
thiamin					🥕
vitamin A					🥕
vitamin B6					🥕
vitamin C					🥕
sugar				🥕	

Good folic acid source

Brussels Sprouts – Fresh / Frozen, Steamed / Cooked / Boiled

1 cup (155.0 grams) = 65 calories

NUTRIENT	NONE	VERY LOW	LOW	HIGH	VERY HIGH
saturated fat			🥕		
cholesterol	🥕				
soduium			🥕		
dietary fiber					🥕
magnesium				🥕	
manganese				🥕	

Brussels Sprouts – Fresh / Frozen, Steamed / Cooked / Boiled (cont'd)

NUTRIENT	NONE	VERY LOW	LOW	HIGH	VERY HIGH
phosphorus				🥕	
potassium				🥕	
riboflavin				🥕	
thiamin				🥕	
vitamin A					🥕
vitamin B6					🥕
vitamin C					🥕
sugar				🥕	

Butternut Squash – Fresh / Frozen, Steamed / Cooked / Boiled

Seedless butternut squash flesh is safe.

This vegetable is an excellent source of potassium and vitamin E.

1 cup (205.0 grams) = 82 calories

NUTRIENT	NONE	VERY LOW	LOW	HIGH	VERY HIGH
saturated fat		🥕			
cholesterol	🥕				
sodium		🥕			
calcium				🥕	
magnesium				🥕	
manganese				🥕	
niacin				🥕	
potassium					🥕
thiamin				🥕	

Butternut Squash – Fresh/Frozen, Steamed/Cooked/Boiled (cont'd)

NUTRIENT	NONE	VERY LOW	LOW	HIGH	VERY HIGH
vitamin A					🥕
vitamin B6				🥕	
vitamin C					🥕
vitamin E				🥕	
sugar				🥕	

Cabbage – Raw

Cabbage is safe.

This vegetable is a great source of iron and antioxidants.

1 cup (89.0 grams) = 22 calories

NUTRIENT	NONE	VERY LOW	LOW	HIGH	VERY HIGH
saturated fat		🥕			
cholesterol	🥕				
calcium				🥕	
dietary fiber					🥕
iron				🥕	
magnesium				🥕	
manganese					🥕
phosphorus				🥕	
potassium				🥕	
thiamin				🥕	
vitamin B6					🥕
vitamin C					🥕
sugar					🥕

Cabbage – Fresh/Frozen, Steamed/Cooked/Boiled

1 cup (150.0 grams) = 34 calories

NUTRIENT	NONE	VERY LOW	LOW	HIGH	VERY HIGH
saturated fat	🥕				
cholesterol	🥕				
sodium			🥕		
calcium					🥕
dietary fiber					🥕
magnesium				🥕	
manganese					🥕
phosphorus				🥕	
potassium					🥕
thiamin				🥕	
vitamin B6					🥕
vitamin C					🥕
sugar					🥕

Carrots – Raw

Carrots are safe.

They add a necessary boost of vitamin A, beta carotene, a whole host of other vitamins and important antioxidants that may help to protect, or even improve, eyesight.

Hustler's first vegetable test involved a carrot. He loves them, raw or cooked.

1 cup (128.0 grams) = 52 calories

Carrots – Raw (cont'd)

NUTRIENT	NONE	VERY LOW	LOW	HIGH	VERY HIGH
saturated fat		🥕			
cholesterol	🥕				
dietary fiber					🥕
manganese				🥕	
niacin				🥕	
potassium					🥕
thiamin				🥕	
vitamin A					🥕
vitamin B6				🥕	
vitamin C					🥕
sugar					🥕

Carrots – Fresh/Frozen, Steamed/Cooked/Boiled

1 cup (156.0 grams) = 54 calories

NUTRIENT	NONE	VERY LOW	LOW	HIGH	VERY HIGH
saturated fat		🥕			
cholesterol	🥕				
dietary fiber					🥕
manganese				🥕	
potassium				🥕	
thiamin				🥕	
vitamin A					🥕
vitamin B6					🥕
vitamin C				🥕	
sugar					🥕

Cauliflower – Raw

Cauliflower is safe.

This vegetable is rich in many vitamins, minerals and antioxidants.

1 cup (100.0 grams) = 25 calories

NUTRIENT	NONE	VERY LOW	LOW	HIGH	VERY HIGH
saturated fat		🥕			
cholesterol	🥕				
dietary fiber					🥕
magnesium				🥕	
manganese					🥕
niacin				🥕	
pantothenic acid					🥕
phosphorus				🥕	
potassium					🥕
riboflavin				🥕	
thiamin				🥕	
vitamin B6					🥕
vitamin C					🥕
sugar					🥕

Cauliflower – Fresh/Frozen, Steamed/Cooked/Boiled

1 cup (124.0 grams) = 28 calories

NUTRIENT	NONE	VERY LOW	LOW	HIGH	VERY HIGH
saturated fat			🥕		
cholesterol	🥕				

Cauliflower – Fresh / Frozen, Steamed / Cooked / Boiled (cont'd)

NUTRIENT	NONE	VERY LOW	LOW	HIGH	VERY HIGH
dietary fiber					🥕
manganese				🥕	
pantothenic acid					🥕
phosphorus				🥕	
potassium				🥕	
riboflavin				🥕	
thiamin				🥕	
vitamin B6					🥕
vitamin C					🥕
sugar					🥕

Celery – Raw

Celery is safe.

Always remove leafy ends and do not fed unripe or yellow stalks.

Celery is a natural diuretic that stimulates urine production and may help eliminate excess fluids, thereby promoting good kidney and urinary tract health. Additionally, celery and celery juice may provide holistic treatment for arthritic pain.

1 cup (120.0 grams) = 19 calories

NUTRIENT	NONE	VERY LOW	LOW	HIGH	VERY HIGH
saturated fat			🥕		
cholesterol	🥕				
sodium					🥕

Celery – Raw (cont'd)

NUTRIENT	NONE	VERY LOW	LOW	HIGH	VERY HIGH
calcium					🥕
dietary fiber					🥕
magnesium				🥕	
manganese					🥕
pantothenic acid				🥕	
phosphorus				🥕	
potassium					🥕
riboflavin				🥕	
vitamin A					🥕
vitamin B6					🥕
vitamin C					🥕
sugar					🥕

Celery – Fresh/Frozen, Steamed/Cooked/Boiled

1 cup (150.0 grams) = 27 calories

NUTRIENT	NONE	VERY LOW	LOW	HIGH	VERY HIGH
saturated fat			🥕		
cholesterol	🥕				
sodium					🥕
calcium					🥕
dietary fiber					🥕
iron				🥕	
magnesium				🥕	
manganese				🥕	
pantothenic acid				🥕	

Celery – Fresh/Frozen, Steamed/Cooked/Boiled (cont'd)

NUTRIENT	NONE	VERY LOW	LOW	HIGH	VERY HIGH
phosphorus				🥕	
potassium					🥕
riboflavin				🥕	
thiamin				🥕	
vitamin A					🥕
vitamin B6					🥕
vitamin C					🥕
sugar					🥕

Cherry Red Tomatoes – Raw

Red, ripe tomato flesh and skin is safe.

The leaves, stems & unripe tomato flesh is toxic. Tomatoes may cause stomach irritation to dogs with sensitive stomachs.

1 cup (149.0 grams) = 27 calories

NUTRIENT	NONE	VERY LOW	LOW	HIGH	VERY HIGH
saturated fat			🥕		
cholesterol	🥕				
sodium			🥕		
dietary fiber					🥕
magnesium				🥕	
manganese					🥕
niacin				🥕	
phosphorus				🥕	
potassium					🥕

Cherry Red Tomatoes – Raw (cont'd)

NUTRIENT	NONE	VERY LOW	LOW	HIGH	VERY HIGH
thiamin				🥕	
vitamin A					🥕
vitamin B6					🥕
vitamin C					🥕
sugar					🥕

Cucumbers – Raw

Ripe cucumber flesh and skin is safe.

1 cup (104.0 grams) = 16 calories

NUTRIENT	NONE	VERY LOW	LOW	HIGH	VERY HIGH
saturated fat			🥕		
cholesterol	🥕				
sodium		🥕			
calcium				🥕	
dietary fiber				🥕	
iron				🥕	
magnesium					🥕
manganese				🥕	
pantothenic acid				🥕	
phosphorus				🥕	
potassium					🥕
riboflavin				🥕	
thiamin				🥕	
vitamin A				🥕	
vitamin B6				🥕	

Cucumbers – Raw (cont'd)

NUTRIENT	NONE	VERY LOW	LOW	HIGH	VERY HIGH
vitamin C					
sugar					

Green Beans – Raw

Green beans are safe.

Snap and cut green beans are great healthy, low-calorie treats high in vitamin C, vitamin K, and manganese. The fiber and roughage aid and promote a healthy digestive system.

1 cup (110.0 grams) = 34 calories

NUTRIENT	NONE	VERY LOW	LOW	HIGH	VERY HIGH
saturated fat		🥕			
cholesterol	🥕				
sodium			🥕		
calcium				🥕	
dietary fiber					🥕
iron				🥕	
magnesium				🥕	
manganese					🥕
niacin				🥕	
phosphorus				🥕	
potassium				🥕	
riboflavin				🥕	
thiamin				🥕	
vitamin A					🥕

Green Beans – Raw (cont'd)

NUTRIENT	NONE	VERY LOW	LOW	HIGH	VERY HIGH
vitamin B6				🥕	
vitamin C					🥕
sugar				🥕	

Green Beans – Fresh/Frozen, Steamed/Cooked/Boiled

My advice is always keep a bag of frozen green beans accessible!

1 cup (135.0 grams) = 38 calories

NUTRIENT	NONE	VERY LOW	LOW	HIGH	VERY HIGH
saturated fat			🥕		
cholesterol	🥕				
sodium		🥕			
calcium				🥕	
dietary fiber					🥕
iron				🥕	
magnesium				🥕	
manganese					🥕
potassium				🥕	
potassium				🥕	
riboflavin				🥕	
thiamin				🥕	
vitamin A					🥕
vitamin B6				🥕	
vitamin C					🥕
sugar				🥕	

Green Sweet Bell Peppers – Raw

Seedless green sweet bell peppers are safe. Do not feed stem or seeds.

1 cup (149.0 grams) = 30 calories

NUTRIENT	NONE	VERY LOW	LOW	HIGH	VERY HIGH
saturated fat			🥕		
cholesterol	🥕				
sodium		🥕			
dietary fiber					🥕
magnesium				🥕	
manganese					🥕
niacin				🥕	
potassium					🥕
thiamin				🥕	
vitamin A					🥕
vitamin B6					🥕
vitamin C					🥕
sugar					🥕

Iceberg Lettuce – Raw

Iceberg lettuce is safe.

1 cup (55.0 grams) = 8 calories

NUTRIENT	NONE	VERY LOW	LOW	HIGH	VERY HIGH
saturated fat		🥕			
cholesterol	🥕				
calcium				🥕	

Iceberg Lettuce – Raw (cont'd)

NUTRIENT	NONE	VERY LOW	LOW	HIGH	VERY HIGH
dietary fiber					🥕
iron				🥕	
magnesium				🥕	
manganese					🥕
phosphorus				🥕	
potassium					🥕
thiamin				🥕	
vitamin A					🥕
vitamin B6				🥕	
vitamin C					🥕
sugar					🥕

Kale – Raw

Kale is safe.

1 cup (67.0 grams) = 34 calories

NUTRIENT	NONE	VERY LOW	LOW	HIGH	VERY HIGH
saturated fat			🥕		
cholesterol	🥕				
calcium					🥕
dietary fiber				🥕	
iron				🥕	
magnesium				🥕	
manganese					🥕
phosphorus				🥕	
potassium					🥕

Kale – Raw (cont'd)

NUTRIENT	NONE	VERY LOW	LOW	HIGH	VERY HIGH
riboflavin				🥕	
thiamin				🥕	
vitamin A					🥕
vitamin B6					🥕
vitamin C					🥕
sugar	🥕				

Good folic acid source

Kale – Fresh/Frozen, Steamed/Cooked/Boiled

1 cup (130.0 grams) = 39 calories

NUTRIENT	NONE	VERY LOW	LOW	HIGH	VERY HIGH
saturated fat			🥕		
cholesterol	🥕				
sodium			🥕		
calcium					🥕
dietary fiber					🥕
iron				🥕	
magnesium				🥕	
manganese					🥕
niacin				🥕	
potassium					🥕
riboflavin				🥕	
vitamin A					🥕
vitamin B6				🥕	
vitamin C					🥕
sugar				🥕	

Peas – Raw

Peas are safe.

1 cup (145.0 grams) = 117 calories

NUTRIENT	NONE	VERY LOW	LOW	HIGH	VERY HIGH
saturated fat		🥕			
cholesterol	🥕				
sodium		🥕			
dietary fiber					🥕
manganese				🥕	
niacin				🥕	
phosphorus				🥕	
thiamin					🥕
vitamin A				🥕	
vitamin B6				🥕	
vitamin C					🥕
sugar				🥕	

Peas – Fresh/Frozen, Steamed/Cooked/Boiled

1 cup (160 grams) = 124 calories

NUTRIENT	NONE	VERY LOW	LOW	HIGH	VERY HIGH
saturated fat		🥕			
cholesterol	🥕				
dietary fiber					🥕
iron				🥕	
manganese				🥕	
thiamin					🥕
vitamin A					🥕

Peas – Fresh / Frozen, Steamed / Cooked / Boiled (cont'd)

NUTRIENT	NONE	VERY LOW	LOW	HIGH	VERY HIGH
vitamin C					🥕
sugar				🥕	

Potatoes – Fresh / Frozen, Steamed / Cooked / Boiled

Potato flesh and skin is safe.

Green plant parts, spores, tubers and sprouts that grow on potatoes are very toxic.

1 cup (156.0 grams) = 136 calories

NUTRIENT	NONE	VERY LOW	LOW	HIGH	VERY HIGH
saturated fat		🥕			
cholesterol	🥕				
sodium		🥕			
potassium				🥕	
vitamin B6				🥕	
vitamin C					🥕

Pumpkin

Canned pumpkin that is not pie filling is safe.

Seedless fresh pumpkin flesh is also safe. Never feed your dog the skin, stem or unripe flesh.

1 cup (245.0 grams) = 83 calories

NUTRIENT	NONE	VERY LOW	LOW	HIGH	VERY HIGH
saturated fat			🥕		
cholesterol	🥕				

Pumpkin (cont'd)

NUTRIENT	NONE	VERY LOW	LOW	HIGH	VERY HIGH
sodium		🥕			
dietary fiber					🥕
iron					🥕
magnesium				🥕	
manganese				🥕	
pantothenic acid				🥕	
phosphorus				🥕	
potassium				🥕	
vitamin A					🥕
vitamin C					🥕
sugar					🥕

Red Sweet Bell Peppers – Raw

Cleaned and seedless red sweet bell peppers are safe.

As with green peppers, stems and seeds must be removed.

1 cup (149.0 grams) = 46 calories

NUTRIENT	NONE	VERY LOW	LOW	HIGH	VERY HIGH
saturated fat		🥕			
cholesterol	🥕				
sodium		🥕			
dietary fiber					🥕
manganese				🥕	
niacin				🥕	
potassium				🥕	

Red Sweet Bell Peppers – Raw (cont'd)

NUTRIENT	NONE	VERY LOW	LOW	HIGH	VERY HIGH
riboflavin				🥕	
thiamin				🥕	
vitamin A					🥕
vitamin B6					🥕
vitamin C					🥕
sugar					🥕

Romaine Lettuce – Raw

Romaine lettuce is safe.

1 cup (47.0 grams) = 10 calories

NUTRIENT	NONE	VERY LOW	LOW	HIGH	VERY HIGH
calcium				🥕	
dietary fiber					🥕
iron				🥕	
vitamin A					🥕
vitamin C					🥕
sugar					🥕

Spinach – Raw

Spinach is safe.

This vegetable has long been viewed as a nutritionally important vegetable, rich in iron and beta carotene. Juice it, steam it, or finely chop it before adding it to your dog's food. Spinach contains high levels of vitamin K, which may aid bone health and growth.

Spinach – Raw (cont'd)

Spinach also contains lutein for eye health and is an excellent source of calcium, fiber, potassium, vitamin A and vitamin B6.

1 cup (30.0 grams) = 7 calories

NUTRIENT	NONE	VERY LOW	LOW	HIGH	VERY HIGH
saturated fat			🥕		
cholesterol	🥕				
sodium				🥕	
calcium					🥕
dietary fiber					🥕
iron					🥕
magnesium					🥕
manganese					🥕
niacin				🥕	
phosphorus					🥕
potassium					🥕
riboflavin					🥕
thiamin					🥕
vitamin A					🥕
vitamin B6					🥕
vitamin C					🥕
zinc			🥕		

Good folic acid source

Spinach – Fresh/Frozen, Steamed/Cooked/Boiled

1 cup (180.0 grams) = 41 calories

NUTRIENT	NONE	VERY LOW	LOW	HIGH	VERY HIGH
saturated fat			🥕		
cholesterol	🥕				
sodium				🥕	
calcium					🥕
dietary fiber					🥕
iron					🥕
magnesium					🥕
manganese					🥕
niacin				🥕	
phosphorus					🥕
potassium					🥕
riboflavin					🥕
selenium				🥕	
thiamin					🥕
vitamin A					🥕
vitamin B6					🥕
vitamin C					🥕
zinc					🥕

Sweet Potatoes – Fresh/Frozen, Baked/Cooked/Boiled

Sweet potato flesh and skin is safe.

1 cup (328.0 grams) = 249 calories

NUTRIENT	NONE	VERY LOW	LOW	HIGH	VERY HIGH
saturated fat		🥕			
cholesterol	🥕				

Sweet Potato – Fresh/Frozen, Baked/Cooked/Boiled (cont'd)

NUTRIENT	NONE	VERY LOW	LOW	HIGH	VERY HIGH
sodium			🥕		
dietary fiber				🥕	
manganese				🥕	
vitamin A					🥕
vitamin B6				🥕	
vitamin C					🥕
sugar				🥕	

Sweet Yellow Corn – Fresh/Frozen, Steamed/Cooked/Boiled

Although corn is safe for dogs to eat, it is not a vegetable. It is a grain, and it is in plentiful supply in almost all commercial dog foods so there is little to no reason to feed corn.

Hustler receives corn only when it is included in pre-packaged frozen vegetable medleys.

1 cup (164.0 grams) = 132 calories

NUTRIENT	NONE	VERY LOW	LOW	HIGH	VERY HIGH
saturated fat		🥕			
cholesterol	🥕				
sodium		🥕			
dietary fiber				🥕	

Zucchini – Raw

Zucchini flesh and skin is safe.

1 cup (113.0 grams) = 18 calories

NUTRIENT	NONE	VERY LOW	LOW	HIGH	VERY HIGH
saturated fat			🥕		
cholesterol	🥕				
dietary fiber					🥕
iron				🥕	
magnesium					🥕
manganese					🥕
niacin				🥕	
phosphorus					🥕
potassium					🥕
riboflavin					🥕
thiamin				🥕	
vitamin A					🥕
vitamin B6					🥕
vitamin C					🥕
zinc				🥕	
sugar					🥕

Zucchini – Fresh/Frozen, Steamed/Cooked/Boiled

1 cup (180.0 grams) = 29 calories

NUTRIENT	NONE	VERY LOW	LOW	HIGH	VERY HIGH
saturated fat		🥕			
cholesterol	🥕				
sodium			🥕		

Zucchini – Fresh / Frozen, Steamed / Cooked / Boiled (cont'd)

NUTRIENT	NONE	VERY LOW	LOW	HIGH	VERY HIGH
dietary fiber					🥕
iron				🥕	
magnesium					🥕
manganese					🥕
niacin				🥕	
phosphorus					🥕
potassium					🥕
riboflavin				🥕	
thiamin				🥕	
vitamin A					🥕
vitamin B6					🥕
vitamin C					🥕
sugar					🥕

Appendix IV
FOODS WITH POTENTIAL HOLISTIC HEALING PROPERTIES CHART

These charts are compiled based on multiple sources that propose these foods may contain holistic healing properties. Although I have only witnessed very effective healing properties of salmon and sweet potatoes, I chose to include all these foods into Hustler's diet. If a vegetable may provide healing, then I'm going to feed it to my dog.

Hustler's seasonal/environmental allergy symptoms include: itching skin, watery eyes, sniffles, pink to red skin in ears. Since he sometimes suffers from *the itchies*, included is a list of homeopathic skin treatments.

Foods To Potentially Help Relieve Allergy Symptoms

Fruits, vegetables and fish sources rich in one or more of the following natural antihistamines or anti-inflammatories: vitamin C, omega-3 & 6 fatty acids and quercetin.

FOOD	INEFFECTIVE	MODERATELY EFFECTIVE	VERY EFFECTIVE
Apples		🐾	
Blueberries	🐾		

Foods To Potentially Help Relieve Allergy Symptoms (cont'd)

FOOD	INEFFECTIVE	MODERATELY EFFECTIVE	VERY EFFECTIVE
Blackberries	🥕		
Broccoli		🥕	
Brussels Sprouts	🥕		
Butternut Squash		🥕	
Cauliflower	🥕		
Green Sweet Bell Peppers	🥕		
Mangos	🥕		
Oranges	🥕		
Pineapples	🥕		
Raspberries	🥕		
Salmon & Salmon Oil			🥕
Sweet Potatoes			🥕
Tuna & Tuna Oil		🥕	

Homeopathic Treatments To Potentially Provide Itch Relief

Dry, itchy skin is very unpleasant. These topical homeopathic remedies may provide your dog itch relief, especially during allergy season. Before attempting home treatments it's important to rule out more serious causes of canine itching such as parasites, fleas, bacterial infections and mites.

Always apply the following treatments to your dog's skin using a clean soft towel or cloth.

Homeopathic Treatments To Potentially Provide Itch Relief (cont'd)

REMEDY	INSTRUCTION
Apple Cider Vinegar Wash	Mix ½ cup apple cider vinegar & ½ water. Effective treatment for itchy footpads.
Aloe Vera	Apply directly.
Calendula Extract	Apply directly.
Fish Oil	Apply directly.
Jojoba Oil	Apply directly.
Oatmeal Bath	Mix oatmeal & water to form a paste. Rub mixture into skin & leave on approximately 10 minutes. Rinse with clean water. Bathe every other day or two to three times a week when allergies flare up.
Tea Tree Oil Solution	Mix ½ cup oil & ½ cup water in spray bottle. Apply one or two sprays twice a day or whenever you see your dog itching.
Vitamin E Oil	Apply directly. Very effective treatment for dry elbows.
Yellow Dock Rinse	Mix 1 tablespoon yellow dock & 2 cups of boiling water. Let cool. Strain plant & use liquid as rinse.

Foods To Potentially Maintain Good Bone Growth & Stave Off Arthritis

Fruits, vegetables and other foods rich in one or more of the following natural anti-inflammatories, antioxidants and dietary minerals: calcium, iron, vitamins A, B, C, D, E & K, and omega-3 fatty acids.

Included are additional protein sources, such as cooked chicken and liver, you may chose to include in your dog's meals.

Foods To Potentially Maintain Good Bone Growth & Stave Off Arthritis (cont'd)

Apples
Asparagus
Broccoli
Brussels Sprouts
Butternut Squash
Cabbage
Carrots
Celery
Chicken
Cottage Cheese
Egg Yolks
Liver
Kale
Oranges
Pears
Salmon
Spinach
Sweet Potatoes
Tuna

"Paws crossed!"

Foods To Potentially Aid In Digestion

Fruits, vegetables and other foods rich in one or more of the following dietary fibers and minerals: niacin, pectin, potassium and water-soluble fibers.

Hustler never experienced digestion issues prior to the diet, and has experienced regular, healthy bowel movements after starting the diet.

REMEDY	BENEFIT
Alfalfa	kidney tonic, laxative, diuretic & blood purifier
Apples	strengthens intestinal muscles to push waste through gastrointestinal tract & helps eliminate waste

Foods To Potentially Aid In Digestion (cont'd)

REMEDY	BENEFIT
Bananas	strengthens muscular system & adds acidophilus bacteria to bowels, which prevents inflammatory bowel disease
Broccoli (steamed or boiled)	rich fiber source - boosts digestion
Brussels Sprouts	stimulates kidneys & pancreas, & cleanses body tissues
Brown Rice	dense fiber source - boosts digestion
Carrots (steamed or boiled)	increases metabolism, helps remove waste & fat deposits, aids in elimination of uric acid & prevents crystallizing
Celery	promotes good urinary tract health, naturally purifies & detoxifies blood
Chicken (boiled)	bland protein source & easily digested
Cottage Cheese	contains natural & supplemental probiotics
Green Beans (steamed or boiled)	rich fiber & potassium source - boosts digestion
Melons	stimulates urination & eliminates toxins
Pears	tones intestinal muscle & thickens stool
Pumpkin (canned, not pie filling)	thickens stool

Foods Considered To Contain Cancer-Preventing Properties

Fruits, vegetables and food sources rich in one or more of the following natural antioxidants: bioflavonoids, carotenoids, chlorophylls, phytochemicals, selenium and vitamin E.

Let me be clear, there are no foods or dietary supplements proven to prevent cancer in dogs. These are foods rich in natural antioxidants considered to contain cancer prevention and cancer-fighting properties.

Foods Considered To Contain Cancer-Preventing Properties (cont'd)

Alfalfa	Liver
Apricots	Mangos
Broccoli	Potatoes
Brussels Sprouts	Pumpkin (canned, not pie filling)
Butternut Squash	Salmon
Cabbage	Spinach
Carrots	Sweet Potatoes
Cauliflower	Tuna

Foods Considered To Benefit Eyes & Vision

Vegetables rich in carotenoids and vitamin A, which are natural antioxidants.

FOOD	BENEFIT
Broccoli	Paws crossed!
Carrots	Paws crossed!

Food Used To Help Stop Stool Eating (Coprophagia)

Yuck, I know. But I wanted to include it in case your dog does it.

Fruits and vegetables rich in either papain, a proteolytic enzyme, or sulfur. Based on multiple sources, a teaspoon or two of pineapple daily is widely accepted and recommended as the best food to stop stool eating.

Brussels Sprouts	Pumpkin (canned, not pie filling)
Cabbage	Spinach
Pineapples	

Appendix V

MY DOG'S TREAT CALORIE TRACKING CHART

Create your own Treat Timetable! Write down your dog's old snack foods and treats, then record all his or her new healthy treats.

Optional: Want to be shocked by how many unnecessary fatty calories your dog once ate? Record your dog's old treats calorie information, then list the new healthy treats calorie information.

For example, here is Hustler's Treat Calorie Tracking Chart:

OLD FATTY TREATS	NEW HEALTHY TREATS	CALORIES SAVED!
5 dry biscuits = 200 calories	14 small carrot bites = 30 calories	170 calories saved & 9 extra treats!
1 dry fatty biscuit = 40 calories	1 large celery stalk = 10 calories	30 calories saved & a crunchy chewfest!
2 dry fatty biscuits = 80 calories	1 cup of chopped apple slices = 65 calories	15 calories saved & 6 more treats!

Start tracking how few calories your dog is eating while he or she snacks more – Download a blank printable version of My Dog's Treat Calorie Tracking Chart online at *www.AmazingTreatDiet.com*

Appendix VI

MY DOG'S WEIGHT LOSS CHART

Track your dog's weight loss and celebrate your achievements!

For example, here is Hustler's Weight Loss Tracking Chart:

DATE	CURRENT WEIGHT	IDEAL WEIGHT	POUNDS TO LOSE	NOTES
1/1/2010	96 lbs	69 lbs	27 lbs	Start diet. Snacks – carrots, pears Meals – added green beans & salmon
2/2010	Unknown – Too afraid to confront scale	69 lbs	Unknown	Able to see a waistline. Shinier coat. Began feeding broccoli, cauliflower & spinach.
3/2010	Unknown	69 lbs	Unknown	Definitely seeing more definition around abdomen. More energetic. Large spinach servings cause gas.
5/2010	69 lbs	69 lbs	0 lbs	We did it! Celebrate with a fresh healthy dinner!

Start tracking your dog's weight loss – Download a blank printable version of My Dog's Weight Loss Chart online at *www.AmazingTreatDiet.com*

For further reading...

The American Society for the Prevention of Cruelty to Animals
http://www.aspca.org

American Kennel Club
http://www.akc.org

Association For Pet Obesity Prevention
http://www.petobesityprevention.com

The Humane Society of the United States
http://www.humanesociety.org

U.S. Food & Drug Administration
http://www.fda.gov

The Dog Bible by Tracie Hotchner
http://www.traciehotchner.com

Thank you for reading our story.
We'd love to hear from you, and hope you'll share your success story with us!

– Katie & Hustler

www.AmazingTreatDiet.com

1949987R00087